Are You Guys Brothers?

by
Brian McNaught

authorHOUSE®

AuthorHouse™
1663 Liberty Drive, Suite 200
Bloomington, IN 47403
www.authorhouse.com
Phone: 1-800-839-8640

First published by AuthorHouse 6/11/2008

ISBN: 978-1-4343-8248-1 (e)
ISBN: 978-1-4343-8246-7 (sc)

Library of Congress Control Number: 2008903574

Printed in the United States of America
Bloomington, Indiana

This book is printed on acid-free paper.

Cover design by
Brian "Briz" Ahern
http://brizycomics.carbonmade.com

ALSO BY BRIAN McNAUGHT

A Disturbed Peace
  Selected Writings of an Irish Catholic Homosexual

On Being Gay
  Thoughts on Family, Faith, and Love

Gay Issues in the Workplace

Now That I'm Out, What Do I Do?
  Thoughts on Living Deliberately

"Sex Camp"

DEDICATION

I dedicate this book to my cherished spouse, best friend, and soul brother,

Ray Struble

and to all those who celebrate with us the love we share.

Fame or integrity: which is more important?
Money or happiness: which is more valuable?
Success or failure: which is more destructive?

If you look to others for fulfillment,
you will never truly be fulfilled.
If your happiness depends upon money,
you will never be happy with yourself.

Be content with what you have;
rejoice in the way things are.
When you realize there is nothing lacking,
the whole world belongs to you.

Tao te Ching

1

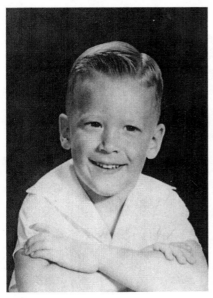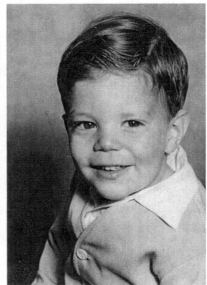

The two gold-framed photographs of us that hang on our bedroom wall make most people smile and sigh appreciatively.

"How cute," they say. "Ray, you look just the same. Brian, look at your chubby cheeks."

Who doesn't delight in the sight of innocence -- so fresh, so wide-eyed and so trusting? It could be small children, like us, grinning in delight, or Labrador puppies, like our Brit, tumbling in a wrestling match, or a single file of fuzzy, yellow ducklings, like those in the canal at the end of our street, paddling hard to keep up with their mother. There seems to be so much potential for happiness in those frozen moments. We all wish them each a lifetime of joy, unscarred by the clumsy, unconscious, selfish behavior of others.

Depending upon our age, we perhaps also look at the sight of such purity with an apprehensive feeling of sadness or regret. I do. Experience tells me that the innocence we see today will eventually be lost. Not completely, perhaps. It depends upon how many kicks are endured and how much support is available. But there are adults who carelessly victimize young, smiling children with chubby cheeks, cars that recklessly run over playful puppies, and snapping turtles that hungrily pull down unsuspecting young ducklings. It's the way of life for most living things.

Ray looks to be three in the photo. I think I'm two. The photos are headshots taken lovingly, proudly, and in my case apprehensively, by our parents. (Terry, the brother born before me, was bitten by the family dog and died at fifteen months, undoubtedly causing my folks great concern for my health and safety.) Each photograph was displayed on our respective family walls or in albums until they were brought together as a pair in 1976 when Ray and I met.

We were handsome children. At the time, one might have wondered what our futures would hold -- marriage and children, or the ministry, financial success, fame, and a long, healthy, happy life of devotion to our parents, our Church, and our country? Relatives and friends must have wished that we could always stay young, and innocent, and happy.

But, we are no longer young, and our innocence was long ago stolen or given away. Nevertheless, we're still both very, very happy, and we both feel that meeting one another in our mid-twenties made that happiness a real possibility in our lives.

In actuality, Ray and I are three years apart, with me being the oldest. In the 1950s, we both were growing up in Midwestern Catholic families of seven children. We were *exceptionally* good boys with ready smiles, polished manners, and an eagerness to please. We both were Altar Boys, Patrol Boys, and Boy Scouts. We both dressed up as priests at home, read the book *Treasure Island* and *Boy's Life* magazine, and watched "Ding Dong School" with Miss Francis, and "Captain Kangaroo" with Mr. Greenjeans. Ray and I both slid down the stairs on our bellies face first, made our First Holy Communions in new blue suits, and later did indeed enter religious life.

Regrettably, we both would also end up in hospital emergency rooms with tubes down our throats, having our stomachs pumped after attempting suicide. We both would be sexually abused by adults. And we both would find ourselves in metal folding chairs at meetings of Alcoholics Anonymous repeatedly telling our stories to other addicts.

Had Ray and I grown up in the same state and town, we might have lived in the same neighborhood and attended the same Catholic church and school, but he was in Wichita, Kansas, and I was in Flint, Michigan, and even if we had lived down the street from one another, we probably wouldn't have been close friends because seven-year-olds rarely hang out with four-year-olds, unless they're brothers. And we're *not* brothers, at least not by birth.

Ray's all-time favorite childhood Christmas gift was an authentic Davy Crockett coonskin hat. Mine was a Jerry Mahoney puppet "with a tie," as I specified in my letter to Santa. Both treasures of our youth were lost when "the things of a child" were set aside, and both were joyfully received again as surprise Christmas presents from one another in our fifties – cherished touchstones for the period of time when we couldn't imagine the incredible cruelty we would endure in our lives.

When we were youngsters, you wouldn't mistake us for brothers. Ray had an angular face, a larger nose, and thick blond hair. My face was round, my nose small, and my hair brown. He looked a lot like his brother, Bob, two years older with whom Ray shared a bedroom. Each Sunday, Bob and Ray were marched down the aisle of Blessed Sacrament church with their other brothers, Rodney, Art, Al, John, and young David. Their very proud parents were farm-raised Kansans, Art, a lean 6'2 shoe store owner, and Mary, his 5'2" bride, to her regret, the only female in the brood.

I shared a bedroom with my younger brother, Tom. For much of my life, he was my best friend.

Bob was my age. Ray was Tom's age. Having close brothers with whom we shared bedrooms, a desk, pets, socks, ties, secrets, and underwear impacted Ray's and my experience and expectations of male friendship and intimacy.

Today, at the ages of 60 and 57, after 32 years as life partners, seven of which have been spent legally in a Vermont civil union, and five spent as married spouses, we are asked repeatedly, in a variety of situations, in most every place in the world that we have visited, "Are you guys brothers?"

There were times when that question perplexed me, times that it angered me, and now it merely amuses me that the person asking the question couldn't have considered other explanations for our mutual love. ("Have you seen *Brokeback Mountain*?")

What the questioner – the flight attendant in London, the salesperson in New York, the street vendor in Vietnam – sees in us, and what they want to define, is great affection. What box does that affection fit into when we're both men, assumedly heterosexual? And the intimacy they see doesn't come from hand-holding, kissing, or other traditional physical displays of affection, though those are essential ingredients of our love. It comes from Ray holding the door for me or me for him; gently guiding the other forward with a hand at the other's back or elbow. It's watching us make sure the other's needs are taken care of – pillow for the flight, water without ice at the table, the first offer of popcorn – that may be confusing to the observer. Heterosexual men, they reason, don't make sustained eye contact, or share salads, or gently tease each other, unless they're brothers.

And yet, if I was having breakfast with my brother Tom, I'd feel much less confident telling the server what he wanted to drink, as he headed to the bathroom. When Bob was dying of cancer a couple of years ago, Ray, who stood vigil at his bedside for the final three weeks of Bob's life, would have felt less sure of himself in shopping for his brother's favorite foods than he would have been in looking for mine. With brothers, even those with whom we are very close, there isn't usually consensus on what television show to watch together, nor ease in how to negotiate different choices in programming. With brothers, there is familiarity but there is also a fiercely-guarded separateness from one another. Not with Ray and me.

So, those two very sweet boys who are pictured together on our bedroom wall, young innocents who by all rights should have been allowed to stay innocent, are not biological brothers. They are more.

We found each other through Dignity, an organization for gay Catholics, and came together as roommates with another Dignity member in a spacious apartment on Beacon Street in Brookline, Massachusetts. It was May 4, 1976. I arrived from Detroit, where I had recently made headlines for being fired by the Catholic diocesan newspaper for affirming that I was gay. Ray and the second roommate, Patrick, knew of my hunger strike and civil rights ordeal in Michigan through coverage in the national, Catholic, and gay press. I had met Patrick at a previous national convention of Dignity, but I hadn't met Ray.

"Stay away from him," I was warned in the friendliest of manners by Dignity's national officers, who were also living at the time in Boston. "He's fragile," they insisted, assuming that I, the "gay activist," was much more toughened by the world.

He didn't look fragile as he excitedly approached my red Opel station wagon that pulled my five by eight U-Haul trailer and all of my life's possessions. He looked handsome – not blond as he was described and as I had imagined – but good looking in his strawberry blond hair, angular face, prominent nose, broad smile and tan trench coat. Handsome, but not really my type.

He and Patrick had waited for me at the Mass. Ave. exit off of the turnpike. We all assumed correctly that I would get lost, so they borrowed a car and waited to spot me. When I pulled over, Ray emerged from their car, waved a big welcome, smiled as he crossed the street, and then carefully entered my car and my life, as my young, spoiled, Irish setter Jeremy defensively barked loudly at him from the back seat.

Despite how extraordinarily wonderful and joyful the ride we have since taken together has ultimately been, sometimes I wonder if Ray would have gotten into my car had he known everything about me and my family, and whether I would have encouraged him to take the seat next to me had I known everything about him and his. Because it wasn't just the good looking 25-year-old Kansan that got into my car that beautiful spring day in Boston, it was all of the pain he'd experienced in his life before I met him, and all of the scars that pain had created in his heart and soul. This gay man that I was saying "hello" to for the first time at age 28 might end up making more than a million dollars a year in salary on Wall Street, but he might also live with the fear that he's "crazy" because his father and brother are. And I may end up being for him a wonderful homemaker, but I also may be uncomfortable being held in bed by him because of the persistent panic in those situations I feel because of childhood sexual abuse. There were, in reality, more than Ray, me and the Irish setter in that car as we followed Patrick down Beacon Street to the third floor, walk-up apartment. Our strict grandparents, our alcoholic fathers, our prudish mothers, our competing siblings, our demeaning coaches, our sexual abusers, and our dismissive employers were also in the back seat. And there was more than my possessions being carted in my U-Haul trailer. There was all of the past and all of the future we might create together. There were all of the influences, both positive and negative, that might further wound and debilitate us *or* might help us help each other in our development into wholesome, healthy, happy men who eventually might learn to recapture the innocence so effectively caught in our childhood photographs. And if we chose to take a ride together, could we successfully do so for very long in a heterosexual culture that feared and fought male/male intimacy and same-sex relationships and in a gay male culture that feared and fought monogamy and commitment? At the time, we were far too young and far too naïve to think about all of that. We were just kids.

2

Everybody's got a story to tell that explains, though doesn't excuse, who and what they have become in life. Look at a menacing, multi-tattooed and pierced, Hells Angels biker, for instance, and imagine what he looked like as a skinny, giggling first grader. Now, wonder what transpired at home, at school, in the neighborhood and in his church to influence the decisions he has made to choose the life he has embraced. He's got a good story to tell. And to fully understand how he became the man he is today, we'd also need to know his parents' stories, and their parents' too.

My paternal grandmother, Edith, for instance, was orphaned at the age of five. Both of her parents and all of her siblings died in the same year of disease. I recall watching my grandmother in her 90s weep from guilt for not having said her prayers the night her mother died.

When she was taken in by her grandparents, Edith's grandmother (whose story I'd love to know) whispered to the five-year-old, "You would have died too if you weren't so evil." My grandmother fled that farmhouse as soon as she was able, which was incidentally true as well for my father, the oldest of her seven children.

I'm not a trained psychologist, but it occurs to me that my father's secretive, lifelong lament that he never got the love and approval that he wanted from his mother, had some impact on his inappropriate sexual behavior with me and whoever else in my family he confused with his unfortunate touch.

My cousin says that her dad, my father's only brother, inappropriately touched her too. There's a link in the story there, but I don't know what it is.

In hearing such things, many people say, "There but for the grace of God go I," but isn't it really, "There but for the luck of circumstances go I"? The idea that the loving God of my life was involved in any way with my father's behavior, my grandmother's behavior, or her grandmother's behavior, is counterintuitive for me. All of them had a story to tell, influenced by a variety of random events. Again, it doesn't excuse their behaviors, but it helps us explain them, and explain me.

So, when Ray got into the car with me in 1976, it wasn't just my story he was encountering, but that of many others, including that of my grandmother, Edith, whom he soon met and charmed. And *my* story was soon influenced by Ray's story, and that of his parents, and of his immigrant great grandparents, one of whom fed the starving local Indians from her kitchen door, despite the protests of her Kansan neighbors.

I wish both sets of our parents were alive today so that we could now ask them more details of their stories. Yet, they were all of a generation in which you didn't talk much about your personal feelings. I remember once asking my mother if she was pregnant with me when my brother Terry died. "Why do you ask such questions?" was her bewildered and pained response. While fishing with my father, I asked him during a lull, "Are you happy with

9

your life, Dad? Do you have any regrets?" I wasn't trolling for an apology for sexual abuse. At the time, I didn't think of our morning showers and Saturday naps during my youth as such. "Why do you ask those kinds of questions?" Waldo (a name he hated) exhaled with exasperation. "I just want to know that you're happy," I replied sheepishly. "Yes, yes," he said. "Now watch your line. You'll never catch any fish with all of this talking."

My folks weren't any more secretive (Mom would say "private") than most of my friends' parents. Immediately after my father's funeral, several smiling men my age and older came up to assure me that my recollections during my eulogy matched their experiences with their fathers exactly. Once when playing Gin Rummy with my card-loving father (a joy I share), I sat and stared at him for a moment as he contemplated his discard. He looked up and said "What?"

"I just want you to know that I love you," I said.

"You think you're going to get a better card from me for that?" he replied with a slight smirk as he discarded, and then broke the moment's awkward silence by saying, "Hurry up. You're holding up the game."

Ray's father was equally non-communicative of his feelings to his seven sons, except for his admonitions on what they weren't doing right. He was the youngest of his family, who married the youngest of hers. Art's family had some money though, where Mary's didn't. Their childhood farm experiences were different in what was expected of their labors.

Ray's dad was a proud man. A sepia photo of him sitting tall in the saddle is on Ray's bedside table. Ray remembers his father as very affectionate until he had his "nervous breakdown." The family lost the shoe business, and was forced to move to a smaller house as Art underwent shock treatment locally. The Struble side, who felt that

Mary was beneath their station, blamed her for his condition. Upon his return home, the formerly confident man in whose long arms Ray and his brothers once felt safe and loved, was now a confused shell of himself who had to be followed around by his seven-year-old son when he took to wandering the neighborhood. With time, and with the numbing help of Peppermint Schnapps, he eventually found his footing and became a successful real estate agent.

Ray, who discovered his sexual attraction for boys at a very early age, left for the seminary at Notre Dame University right after high school. My father had done the same, though not to the Holy Cross order. Both men stayed in the seminary for a short time, both worked themselves through college upon their departure from religious life, and both became very successful businessmen, Dad at General Motors, and Ray at Lehman Brothers. That is undoubtedly why my father found much more to discuss with Ray than he did with me. He always felt that I was wasting my talent as a writer and educator on gay issues. It was only when I started getting invited to speak about gay issues to senior management at major corporations such as Ford and Chrysler that my work life presented him something to which he could relate.

Mary Gorman Struble, like my mother Mary Virginia Day McNaught, was a very devout Catholic, active in women's auxiliary groups, and overseer of her brood's religious practices. My mother was a princess too, the only daughter among five children of a stern, Protestant, Detroit-based electrician and his second generation Irish Catholic wife. My father, in turn, spoiled his bride, as did Art with Mary.

My older sister Kathy taught me to dance, a few years before Ray's mom taught him. My father gave me "the sex talk," such

11

as it was. Mary did a better job with Ray, (but from a woman's perspective.)

My mother didn't talk about sex until her children were all grown and full of opinions of their own. She was an exceedingly modest woman, prudish by today's standards, as was my father's mother. The latter, according to family lore, was never seen naked by my grandfather. The same cannot be said for my mother with me. When I was in fourth grade, playing "fort" in their Grand Blanc, Michigan dressing room closet, my mother and I traumatized each other with my unintended view of her naked entry into the bathroom for a late morning shower.

"You *dirty* little boy," she said angrily without thinking. "What are you doing? Get out of here!" That was an important, painful part of my story when Ray got into my car for the first time. What of my mother's own story would prompt such a horribly inappropriate response to her mortified and frightened nine-year-old son? (Had she at that moment only recalled and understood the meaning of the collage of photos of near naked wrestlers on my bedroom walls, she would have known that seeing her naked was not my objective in being in her closet.)

Ray's and my childhood stories have a few details that some people may find unsettling and not particularly flattering to us or to our families. For many, many years, Ray and I withheld such details from our stories because we both wanted to make a good impression on others. But there is no explanation or understanding of our lives if the stories we tell are without the full truth.

The truth be told, though, the emotional or psychological challenges that all of our parents and grandparents experienced, were not the most powerful influences in either Ray's or my life.

Though we both have been adversely impacted by the imperfections of our primary caregivers, who hasn't been?

The reason that it took me many years to name what happened between my father and me as sexual abuse is that I really fashioned myself as the product of a Kennedyesque childhood. I was well sheltered, fed, clothed, educated, and loved by an extended family. So, too, was Ray. We both have happy memories of birthdays, Christmas, Thanksgiving, Halloween, and Easter. That's not to say there wasn't too much drinking or high drama at such times, but I've yet to meet a person with accurate Hallmark recollections of their family holidays.

We both have positive feelings about our Catholic education, our religious instruction, and our childhood experiences of the Church. We feel enriched by our early introduction to mystery and ritual. I'm not saying that today we don't feel emotionally and spiritually abused by the institutional Church, but that's another story.

I don't believe in fate, nor do I imagine there is a great puppeteer in the sky. To do so would force me to acknowledge that God likes me better than God likes people who haven't experienced the joy and satisfaction that I have found in my life with Ray. So, I don't know exactly how to explain how these two young men, one from Wichita and one from Detroit, ended up in the same car and the same storyline. But I'm very, very grateful. So, too, is Ray

3

We're not each other's types, Ray and I. At least, we weren't when we first met, and for the first few years of our relationship. I wasn't attracted to blonds or brunettes. For some unknown reason, I zeroed in on the Mediterranean look – dark hair on head and chest, masculine and cocky. I was also attracted to older men than me. My first partner, an Episcopal priest, lacked the hairy chest, but he weakened my knees when he leaned up against me in his leather jacket at the "Woodward" bar in Detroit. I was 23. He was 38. We lived together for a couple of years until I got past my sexual excitement long enough to realize I was in an emotionally abusive relationship.

Harville Hendrix, a favorite of Oprah's, says in his book *Getting the Love You Want* that we are attracted to the shadows of our primary caregivers in order to work out unresolved childhood issues. Father Dan's emotional detachment mirrored my own father's, as did his inability to give approval. That was probably what kept me in his life for so long – my hope for his approval.

If Hendrix is right, Ray is the shadow of my mother, which is perhaps why I have always felt such comfort with him, but not the initial crazy sexual charge I have had with others who were my physical-attraction type.

Pheromones apparently have a lot to do with sexual charge. I don't fully understand it, but I know that sometimes even the type of person who would usually attract you doesn't turn you on, and then, surprisingly with another person, you get sexually excited just *talking* to them. The chemicals in your brain allegedly trigger a response to the chemicals being emitted by the other person's brain. Their body chemistry – scent, skin temperature, or "aura," – turns you on. As my friend Mary Lee Tatum used to say, you feel like Woody Woodpecker. When he sees a pretty female woodpecker, his eyes roll around, he drools, and his brains fall out. Being "turned on" is intoxicating and can be emotionally paralyzing. If you have an addictive personality like mine, you have little defense.

Though we weren't initially each other's type, for many years Ray and I had a very satisfying sexual relationship. Allowing for the ups and downs of erotic charge that every couple goes through, we were both very satisfied with the amount, the variety, and the intensity of our love-making. Eventually, I came to see Ray as the most handsome man in the world, at least in my world. He *became* my type, and I began to compare all other men to him. (I still do.) As is true for all couples, gay or straight, our sexual activity with each other was impacted by a variety of factors – work, stress, alcohol and drugs, hormone levels, physical ability, childhood experiences, input from others, and boredom with repetition. Nevertheless, neither of us felt deprived.

The drug Celexa has taken its toll on Ray's erections today, and Cialis and Viagra cause him a stuffed up head that makes sex less than appealing. Ray's sexual drive is also now very low. Mine continues to be very high. In the past, we tried an extended threesome relationship for awhile to address our sexual and emotional frustrations but found that my double standard jealousy and the third party's keener interest in Ray made it untenable. Masturbation, or self-pleasuring, and an occasional "Happy Ending" massage are my sexual outlets now. Ray couldn't care less.

But at 60, as fun and as wonderfully fulfilling as an orgasm with Ray can be, it's not an essential ingredient of our happiness. Instead, we consistently greet each other with big, loving smiles throughout the day, we hold hands in bed when we watch television, we occasionally walk with an arm around the other as we take a nightly stroll down Commercial Street in Provincetown or Las Olas Boulevard in Ft. Lauderdale, we hold one another and kiss in the hot tub, we rub moisturizing cream on each other's hard-to-reach areas of the back, we join hands for an acknowledgment of our good fortune before every meal, we kiss good morning, goodbye, and goodnight each day, and we cuddle in cold weather. We make love, but we don't have sex. Thus, today we're more HOMosexuals than we are homoSEXuals. And that's okay with us both.

Our first sexual encounter was initiated by us playing footsies as we watched television with an afghan thrown over us on the sofa. Patrick, who sat in a nearby chair, was oblivious that the first stage of mating was underway.

Neither Ray nor I wanted to be in a committed relationship. We both had just ended partnerships, he with a man with whom he had left the seminary, and me with a man who had helped me start the Detroit Dignity chapter. Both separations were painful and neither of us, in the "wisdom" of our mid-to-late twenties, wanted to be hurt or confined again. After all, it was the 1970s and the gay civil rights movement was indistinguishable from the sexual liberation movement. Aids was a misspelled gas reliever. Bathhouses were respectable and popular. Monogamy was considered "white bread" boring and counter-revolutionary.

But Ray and I became instant soul mates. We shared a spiritual hunger, we shared values, and we shared a commitment to issues of social justice. We both read books by Thomas Merton and Alan Watts. We both cherished honesty, thoughtfulness, generosity, courtesy, and good order. When I was securing my status as a conscientious objector to the war in Vietnam, Ray was helping black Southerners register to vote.

He, like me, was a hard worker, and a thoroughly decent man who endeared himself immediately to my dog Jeremy, to my younger brother Tom, (who moved in with us for six months,) and to my grandmother, Edith, and my Aunt Joan, who shared a home in nearby Bedford, MA, and owned a cottage on Pleasant Pond near Deerfield, NH.

Everything I liked, Ray liked, including my cooking. And he enjoyed washing dishes. We were a great team.

Like my mother, he was gentle and kind. He complained little and smiled a lot. He was playful and considerate, and a person of great integrity.

Unlike my mother, Ray smoked and drank as much as I did. And he *loved* to dance. We would sometimes go out to gay bars to dance, but just as often the two of us would dance together in the living room, something we continue to do today when music from a film or television program starts our toes tapping, our hips swaying, and our fingers snapping. We spontaneously jump up from our sacred perches and do everything from a waltz and polka to hip hop and rap. At the Wall Street wedding in the Hamptons of a beloved nephew and his beautiful bride, we were on the dance floor for nearly every song, fast and slow, with Ray always allowing me to lead. He's centered that way – no silly preoccupations with what behaviors are construed as masculine.

The footsies under the afghan led to secretive sex that night in one of our bedrooms at the back of the apartment that were joined by a glassed-in porch. We didn't want to hurt Patrick's feelings, as we had spoken of ourselves as a "family" from the day I moved in, and one might argue that being a family would mean doing *everything* together. But neither of us was sexually interested in Patrick and neither wanted him to feel left out, so we closed the doors and didn't speak of it the next morning.

Kissing was a really integral element of the intimacy we created with one another. Passionate kissing by two men seems to be the most threatening homosexual activity to many heterosexual men. They can laugh about dropping the soap in the shower, but not about two guys locking lips. Yet, if there's no kissing in a love-making scene, I get bored, whether or not I'm a participant. If Ray hadn't been a good kisser, we probably would never have ended up getting married in Canada during our 28th year together.

We kissed a lot during the first several months of our time together, but always as gay guys who had no intention of entering a long-term, committed relationship. We each wanted our freedom to have sex with others and to not get emotionally entangled with feelings of jealousy. And, we both failed in that regard completely.

Patrick was still none the wiser about the status of our relationship. But it was clear to everyone that Ray and I were becoming "very close friends." We all shared house and car expenses and responsibilities in the apartment, including walking Jeremy each morning and night, and we brought Patrick with us wherever we went, but all things weren't equal. Ray and I were daily creating an intimacy that Patrick didn't share.

It was however, an intimacy that dare not speak its name, at least not to one another. I was the more fiercely independent. Today, Ray would say that he was sure he wanted to be in a committed relationship with me after those first couple of months, but I was extremely cautious. It was great to be with him, but I, the budding "gay activist," intellectually sought a new social order in which no one would ever feel confined by guilt and traditional concepts of relationship.

I felt as if I had always been the *good* boy, "a prince of a boy," proclaimed Sr. Claire Marie, IHM, my eighth grade teacher, "the best little boy in the world." I entered a relationship soon after I came out as gay, and went from one monogamous partnership to another. Gay newspapers and magazines at the time were filled from cover to cover with pictures of handsome, masculine gay men who were physically "hot" and seemed ready for sex. Our peer group, including Patrick, had multiple sexual partners. I really, really liked

Ray and really enjoyed the sex we had, but I now wanted to let the "whore" within me loose, if even for just a little while, so that my sex life might not feel so much like vanilla ice cream, predictable and ordinary. And, maybe I'd even find my physical type.

So, one night, I went to the Club Baths. It was immediately after seeing the film *The Omen*, which was not very smart. I carried enough Catholic guilt around with me at the time to make initiating sex with a stranger sufficiently difficult without strutting my stuff with images of the Prince of Darkness on my mind. I went with a friend, who had accompanied Ray and me to the movie. Ray headed home, but sent me off with encouragement. "Go have fun," he said.

I nervously walked around the maze, wrapped around the waist in a towel, for over an hour, hoping that someone, *anyone,* would ask me to have sex. I was too afraid to initiate it. That was true with my father too. I enjoyed our showers and our naps, but I was always afraid to ask for what I wanted. That's one reason I was attracted to the Episcopal priest and to other older men. I figured they would know what they were doing and would take the lead. At an early point in my young gay life, I even reasoned that if I didn't *initiate* the sex, I wasn't morally *responsible* for the behavior. If I waited for someone else to ask, it also meant I would never feel rejected. Unless of course, no one asked.

But one man did ask, and though he wasn't my type, I had a quick, stand up, body-rubbing sexual experience with him. "Okay, time to go home." As my movie-going friend and I were leaving the baths, I pointed out to him the man with whom I had sex. "You're lying," he said. "So did I!"

After a couple more equally frustrating sexual encounters, for which alcohol was generously used to make me less afraid and self-conscious of my body, I headed home to Birmingham, Michigan for

Christmas with my folks. While there, I called Ray in Wichita and invited him to fly to Detroit before heading back to Boston. I picked him up at the airport, gave him a hug and a kiss, and opened his door. Once inside, as I headed down I-94, I said to him, "Why don't you move over closer and sit beside me?"

"That's when I knew he had decided to be in a relationship with me," Ray confides to friends today. "Everything changed after that." And it did.

4

Visiting Paul Shanley in prison is a pleasure for Ray and me, but it's not without its pain. He is our friend, a valued member for thirty-four years of our extended family, a former intimate of us both, and a source of enormous spiritual inspiration at a critical time in each of our lives. For Ray it was Paul creating the "Exodus" Mass for gay Catholics at which Ray played the guitar. For me, it was Paul flying to my defense in Detroit to preach at a "Mass of Solidarity" during my hunger fast in 1974. Right-wing Catholics stormed the altar and unfurled a banner during the homily that read "A moral wrong can never be a civil right." Paul was undaunted. Standing tall and proud, he dismissed the intruders with a quip as they were being dragged from the altar by a group of gay Vietnam vets. He then calmed the shaken attendees and guided us all back to our great feelings of strength and of community.

Driving from Provincetown the long distance to the state penitentiary in Bridgewater, filling out paperwork each time, being thoroughly searched for contraband, waiting sometimes for forty minutes to be admitted or to have Paul join us in the meeting room, buying him salads, cheeseburgers, ice cream and other infrequently-enjoyed foods from the vending machine, and spending an hour or two catching up on each other's lives is a very small token of our appreciation for the mentoring he gave us as we struggled to reconcile our Catholic faith with our sexual attractions. We worry about the safety and physical health of our longtime friend and frequent house guest, and we want him to feel as if he is still an important part of a family that loves him, despite whether or not he is guilty of the crime for which he has been convicted.

But maintaining contact through regular letters and seasonal visits with our controversial friend doesn't sit well with all others, including some family and community members. The 77-year-old Boston diocesan priest, who is viewed by many people as the epicenter of the pedophilia scandal in the U.S. Catholic Church, should be, according to some, disdained, repudiated, and ostracized by us with as much contempt as he has received from his former spiritual shepherds, the bishops of Boston. Not one representative of the archdiocese has visited Paul during his civil punishment, except to insist that he resign his priesthood. Such complete abandonment is called for, according to many, even if the person was once considered a good friend or family member.

What is due a friend or family member with regard to forgiveness? When Jesus counseled us to visit those in prison, did he mean that we should spend time with only the innocent or the accused perpetrators of certain but not all crimes? Like the ritual of going through one's address book at the end of December and deciding which family members and friends you want to keep in your life with a holiday card, this issue raises many feelings and questions.

For instance, what is "family," and what is a "friend?" How are the two different or are they the same? These questions are particularly poignant ones for the gay, lesbian, and bisexual people we know, some of whom were rejected by one or both parents, siblings, and some longtime heterosexual friends. Is "family" *bio*logical or can family be better thought of as *logical*?

We know gay and lesbian people who merge their entire lives with those of their biological family. Holidays and birthdays, and even some vacations, are shared with parents, siblings, nieces and nephews. Some gay couples, we know, even separate from one another to be with their biological families, rather than their "logical" families, at Christmas or Hanukkah. This always strikes us as very strange and a bit sad.

Except for the first Christmas, when we weren't yet a couple, Ray and I have never been away from each other on the holidays. We can't imagine doing so. And while many of our initial Christmas Eves were shared with my grandmother and aunt in their home, we have otherwise always been the host for, or the guest of, our logical family of friends for all significant celebrations of our lives, including our civil union in Vermont and our marriage in Ottawa.

My parents were exceedingly gracious when Ray flew to Detroit from Wichita to spend the remainder of Christmas with us that first year we were together. When I confirmed he was coming, Mom immediately ran out and bought him a stained glass bird window ornament. For many years, it hung in the bedroom as a reminder of her thoughtfulness.

Ray was delighted with and completely enchanted by my family. It felt so warm and welcoming to him, particularly in contrast to the harsh judgment and rejection over his homosexuality that he initially received from his own folks. There was no reservation in my home. Our friends were *always* welcome. The affirmation of Ray as a gay person by my parents and siblings meant a great deal to him and to me, and it gave my relationship with him, and my relationship with them, a wonderful boost.

While my mom and dad and Ray's mom and dad were alive, we were very attentive sons, hosting their visits to the East Coast, visiting the McNaughts in Florida or Michigan, and the Strubles in Kansas. We called them each week, sent cards on all special occasions, and overwhelmed them with gifts at Christmas. When my older brother Michael died in his St. Louis home in a horribly tragic Father's Day gun accident, we surprised my very grateful folks by returning to their home in Michigan after we had flown back to our home in Boston following the funeral. We wanted to ensure that they found their footing in the days that followed the devastating loss of their first born. Ray and I were good sons who were great sources of comfort to our parents. Being essential parts of our biological families was exceedingly important to us.

But, our homosexuality was something that both sets of parents took a long, long time to *fully* accept. My folks were initially much more accommodating than Ray's. They were always genuinely gracious, but they often wished out loud that my life had turned out differently. As wonderful a man as they found Ray to be, they felt that if I had married a woman I would have made a great father. My career choice as an educator on gay issues was a big disappointment, particularly to my dad. And my public homosexuality and frequent appearances in the media was socially embarrassing to them both.

Dad felt I was wasting my talent as a writer and speaker on gay issues. "When are you going to write about something else?" he asked in response to one of my first books, *On Being Gay*. "Why not make this thing you're doing an *avocation* rather than your vocation? You could make a lot of money and *give* it to the gay community."

"What exactly is it, Brian, that I should tell my friends that you do?" Mom politely queried.

But they always remembered Ray's name, which Ray's folks didn't with mine, they never prayed out loud that God would send the right women into our lives, as Ray's dad did once, and they always understood and affirmed that Ray's and my financial futures were shared, which escaped Ray's folks from time to time. That could have been because Ray made a lot more money in his Wall Street position than I did writing a syndicated column in the gay press. Had our incomes been reversed, the positions of our parents might have been as well.

Our friends, on the other hand, always fully celebrated Ray's and my relationship, were very proud of my books, videos, and presentations, and they never questioned what they should say to others about us.

On his deathbed, my father instructed me to "take care of your sisters." He hadn't taken care of his five sisters, other than to stay on varying good terms with them, but he was worried about his two single-parent daughters and he wanted my commitment to watch out over them.

I did so gladly, with Ray's help and hard-earned money, especially with my younger sister, the mother of two young boys, who was often in need of financial help. But as Ray and I were paying her health insurance, her mortgage or her large credit card debts, she was finding emotional solace in a fundamentalist church and was voting for George W. Bush not once but twice, saying cavalierly, "It's not going to kill anyone if he gets elected." This she did despite my persistent, impassioned pleading that Bush's positions on gay marriage and on the morality of homosexuality were completely at odds with Ray's and my life together.

After Bush's astounding and very depressing re-election, I wrote my younger sister, whom I loved and constantly worried about, to say that I no longer felt obliged to be financially supportive of her. In fact, it was then that Ray and I changed our wills so that all of our assets would go to charities at the time of our deaths. My sister was astonished that I would end our relationship over a vote.

I wasn't *ending* our relationship, I explained. It had just become clearer to me that we weren't friends. We were family members. They just aren't the same.

"I will always love you as my sister and share with you the memories of our childhood, but we are not friends. Friends," I suggested, "are people with whom you feel safe and valued. Friends support you, and affirm you, and fight against anything and anyone that might threaten you."

I still send occasional e-mail messages and cards, and make calls to my sister and to all other family members on special occasions, but I no longer identify them all as my friends. When I imagine my funeral and I think of who I would want sitting in the front row or positioned in the first car of the traditional procession (should I have such a service), I want my circle of dear, close friends afforded the privilege of being up front, not those with whom I just shared childhood memories. Sometimes they are the same people, but frequently, they are not.

And if there was to be a priest on an altar (though that is *not* in my plans either), I would much prefer to have Paul Shanley speaking on my behalf, and on behalf of my life of faith, than I would an ordained family member or priest-friend of the McNaughts or of the Strubles, who would, quite possibly, as one family friend did at my sweet mother's funeral, take the occasion to speak of sin.

I know that good friends come and go in our lives. Ray and I have had some very close, close friends with whom we are no longer in touch. I think that is true for everyone, gay or straight. And I know that one's family, despite how alienated from each other you might become, shares a bond of blood that is "thick." They will always be there, but not necessarily *for* you.

Many years ago, in a self-help workshop in which I participated, the group was given a picture of concentric circles and asked to place the names of the people closest to us in the smallest center circle, and the names of those less close, but nevertheless significant in our lives, in the ever-widening circles. The names of family members and friends that I put in the smallest circles then are very different than the ones I would put in today.

The names I would put in the smaller circles today are the ones I would call if something bad happened to Ray, or I would want Ray to call if something bad happened to me. The names in the inner circles are the ones I now call with news of some personal or professional success I have experienced, because I know they will be thrilled for and proud of me. There's no room for jealousy or envy in my inner circles.

My inner circle names are the ones of the people who I know share my values. For instance, there aren't any socially conservative Republicans or "gay-intolerant" religious fundamentalists in my innermost circles. Nor are there people who litter, who are rude to salespeople or cruel to animals, who tell ethnic or sexist jokes, who are stingy, who can't forgive or say "I'm sorry," who drink too much or take recreational drugs, who don't clean up after their dogs, or who have big muscles but no sense of humor about themselves.

Ray is, of course, at the very center of my smallest circle. He's my spouse, my lover, and my brother. Other people continue to come and go from the other small circles. Right now, I'm lucky enough to have a handful of really special friends with whom I feel very safe and valued. They truly are my family.

I'm extremely grateful for all of the people in my life who over the years have allowed and encouraged me to grow into the person I am today. My younger sister, who I still think about a lot, has been one of them. I have come to forgive her for not supporting me in the way I asked and expected her to do. She is my family too, and I love her, even if I feel we're still not friends. One day perhaps we will be. I don't rule out that possibility. In fact, I hope for it.

Our friend Paul Shanley is also one of those people who enabled me to grow to be the person I am today too, and his name is still among those in my inner circle. Maybe we're not *best* friends anymore, but we're most definitely family, regardless of what anyone else says or thinks. It's just logical.

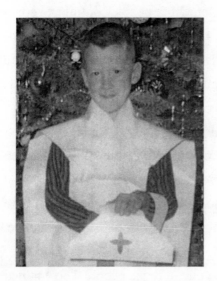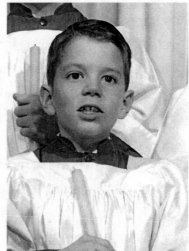

5

During a very large and highly-charged Gay Pride rally in the Boston Commons in 1978, right after the much-publicized, agonizing defeat of gay civil rights legislation in Miami at the hands of Anita Bryant, the keynote speaker, a local anarchist history professor, dramatically, in the heat of his rhetoric, threw a Bible into a burning cauldron. Prompted by the horrified jeers from most of the crowd, including from Ray and me, the rally organizers asked me to speak in response to his defiant, sacrilegious gesture. I chastised him from the stage for abusing a book that had great spiritual significance to the majority of us in attendance, and for resorting to a Nazi tactic to make his point. My comments were enthusiastically welcomed by most of the people in the crowd.

Thirty years later, I have to admit that if it happened again, I would be far less offended, and perhaps even amused by the professor's theatrics. My offense today would come from his complete insensitivity to the feelings of religious gay men and women. My amusement would result from his utter audacity. It was harder for Ray and me then, than it is today, to laugh confidently at the inappropriate behavior of other gay people.

Yet, the speaker did get everyone's attention and he provided me with a terrific benchmark to gauge my feelings about the Bible and other objects considered sacred by many people, such as the image of Mohammed, the American flag, and the consecrated host.

In my family's home, and in Ray's too, the Bible was far more important, but much-less used, than the dictionary. If it was to be handled, it would be done so with great respect. It was a holy book, the word of God. One wouldn't dare write in the Bible other than to record births and deaths in the designated areas in its front or back pages. There would never be words underlined in pen or notations made in the margin. What needed emphasis or explanation was determined by the publisher, who did so with different colored inks and copious footnotes.

While the Old Testament never much held my interest, the words of Jesus, found in red type in the four Gospels, and a small handful of inspired writings by Paul, created my concept of God and guided my spiritual development. The Sermon on the Mount, in particular, seemed to me the crux of the book.

The Jesus that Ray and I met in the writings of the four evangelists was an amazing man, unlike any other in our lives. He was strong, tender, thoughtful, wise, non-judgmental, self-sacrificing, inclusive, focused, loving and forgiving. As such, we and Jesus became really good friends; the best of friends, even. He was nothing at all like the scary Frankenstein Jesus that has been put together clumsily but calculatedly by those who need a monster to enforce their fear-based biases. The Jesus with whom we both built an intimate relationship

31

in our childhoods was a lover, not a hater. He was so cool, he could have been (and perhaps was) gay.

Although I didn't memorize and quote biblical passages as a child, or read the "Good Book" from cover to cover, I was, by Catholic standards, a passionate disciple of Christ. When I watch programs such as *Jesus Camp*, the Oscar-nominated documentary in 2006 on the frightening extreme emotionalism of fundamentalist children, I see myself and the frenzy I could get into as a young Christian. The parents of my neighborhood friends at one time called my mom with the request that I quit trying to convert their children to Catholicism. In high school, I got the highest score they had ever recorded for social work in a standardized career preference test. ("Would you rather read a book to a sick friend than play outside?" Yes.) Though they took my name off the plaque when I identified myself as gay eight years later, I was the unanimous choice of the faculty for the Christian Leadership Award when I graduated from Brother Rice High School in 1966. At Marquette University in Milwaukee, Wisconsin, I was teasingly called "the dorm Catholic" because I went to Mass every day. Shortly after college, I wrote to U.S. Senator Phil Hart (D-MI) and told him in the strongest possible terms that the Holy Spirit had told me he should run for President of the United States. (He did not run, and to my great relief today, never responded to my letter.)

I was an Altar Boy. I can recite from memory the Acts of Contrition, Faith, Hope, and Love, all of which I dutifully learned as a child. I still know by heart the Seven Gifts of the Holy Spirit. I was in a monastery for a short period of time. I went to Catholic schools for sixteen years. I worked at a Catholic newspaper for four years. I started a chapter of a gay Catholic organization and became the group's National Director of Social Action. I taught religious

32

education to school children after work. I won the Catholic Press Association's award for Best Magazine Article of the Year. During my 17-day hunger strike and civil rights battle with the archdiocese, I was compared by one national Catholic columnist to saints of the Church. And, I advised the National Council of Churches and the United States Conference of Bishops on issues facing young adults. No one questioned my Catholic credentials. Thus, I was the perfect person to ask to ascend the stage and quiet the crowd that day when the Bible was burned in effigy.

Yet that same book in our home today is much less cherished than the dictionary, which makes sense because, from our perspective now, the Bible is a primary source of barbaric behaviors toward homosexuals, while the dictionary helps us on a daily basis to answer important questions. Beyond gay-bashing, the so-called "good book," to us, is one of the two chief sources of justification of the world's most evil actions. (The other is the Koran.) Rather than being a bridge to salvation, the book, as it is used, in our opinion, is more a major roadblock to the peace that Jesus promised us if only we would live our lives as he lived his.

The stories of the Old Testament, I feel, even if accurately recorded, trap people in cultural contexts that have nothing to do with their daily lives. Though written generally with the best of intentions, the Bible is an enormous cause of abuse - spiritually, emotionally, and physically – to gay people, women, people of color, Jews, and Muslims, among others. It and the Koran are the most inappropriately cited sources ever written. In the tortured lives of many people, the Bible is certainly not sacred, and therefore burning it is not sacrilegious. Doing so publicly might be really stupid, particularly during a national gay civil rights struggle when you're trying to convince heterosexuals that you share many of their values. But, it's not, in my view today, sacrilegious.

If other books can be burned, so too can the Bible. I would prefer not to cause emotional chaos in someone else's life by doing so, just as I wouldn't throw darts at a picture of the homophobic "saint" Pope John Paul II in front of devout Polish nuns, burn the American flag in front of my Reagan-loving father, or mock Mohammed in front of a fundamentalist Muslim. But the Bible is not beyond criticism and burning it, in my opinion, is far less abusive of it than misusing it to justify one's biases.

Do I wish I hadn't chastised the professor for burning the Bible? What I wish was that I hadn't been so personally horrified by his actions. My emotional reaction was irrational, bordering on hysterical, like the young fundamentalist children in *Jesus Camp*. Why do we cling with so much fear to such "things" for meaning?

If the future of the world depends on any or all of us believing that Moses brought down the mountain tablets personally inscribed by God, or that Jesus rose from the dead, or that Mary assumed into Heaven in her earthly body, or that Joseph Smith met an angel in America who gave him golden tablets, or that Mohammed ascended into Heaven in a chariot pulled by winged horses, I think that we're in big, big trouble. And if we can't challenge religious mythology openly, and laugh about it if we find it funny, then, Zeus bless us, we're in far worse spiritual and emotional shape than we might imagine.

Nothing should be taboo to discuss, if necessary outside the range of children. Ray and I cringe when we hear the word "nigger" but we recoil even further when we *read* "the n word." We hate the word "faggot," but please don't start referring to it as "the f word."

Such behavior gives a simple word or event more power than we can possibly manage.

Is nothing sacred then? I do feel that some things ought to be protected at all costs. But they're not made of paper, cloth, bread, or stone. They're ideas, like perhaps the ones that each of us has the responsibility to work toward creating a world where every person is adequately clothed, sheltered, fed, and educated, that children have a right to their innocence, and that no one should be victimized because they are different. Why isn't it considered sacrilegious that we expend so little time, money, and thought on these worthy endeavors? How can we spend millions of dollars every year to fight *or* to defend gay marriage, rather than investing that enormous amount of money in feeding and clothing the world's desperately needy? These are burning questions for Ray and for me.

6

"If I could give you a pill that would make you a heterosexual, would you *choose* to take it?"

The syndicated television talk show host was not being hostile. He was genuinely interested in better understanding the lives of gay people in his 1974 interview of me. The underlying question is "Do you like being gay, or would you choose to be straight?" Even more precisely, the question is, "Are you happy?"

When I told my parents that I was gay, my mother cried and said in great pain, "Brian, the world is going to be awful to you and there's nothing I can do to protect you."

She was right. Some people in the world would choose to be truly awful to me – death threats, harassing phone calls, obscene mail, open hostility during my college and corporate presentations, cruel comments in the press, icy silence from some formerly-close family members and friends – and there was nothing she could do to protect me, other than to remind me from time to time that she loved me, and be angered by how others, both straight and gay, responded so meanly to her sensitive middle child. But since coming out publicly at the age of 26 in 1974, I've never wanted, no matter how bad it got, to take a pill that would make me a heterosexual, if such a pill existed.

Ray and I have absolutely no regrets. We're gay men who truly and fully celebrate being who and what we are. We see being gay as a special gift to us, and we feel that we've had incredibly joyful, satisfying, and meaningful lives. We're very, very happy being gay and we wholeheartedly wish that were true for *all* gay men and women in the world. But we sadly acknowledge that it isn't.

On the Fourth of July each year in Provincetown, the magical spit of sand at the tip of Cape Cod on which we have the privilege of living during the summer, head-turning muscular young gay men from throughout the country promenade shirtless down Commercial Street, showing off their hard work at the gym, but doing so, in most instances, without a single smile. If Ray and I try to make eye contact with, and smile at them, most of them will disdainfully look away, as if we were foolishly coming on to them sexually. Yet, we're only trying to say, "Welcome to Provincetown."

I have often wondered why so many of them, from our perspective, look to be so unhappy, these formerly scrawny "sissies" who have pumped themselves up with weights and steroids. Perhaps they *are* happy and don't want to show it. Ray and I have speculated that maybe there's a secret "tribal" understanding that happy faces, except when induced by recreational drugs, are not considered masculine and sexually provocative.

We've had a similarly sad and lonely experience with some gay men dressed in leather and with many college-age lesbians, both groups of which also have a designated week in this spectacularly beautiful "safe harbor" of humanity. The young women excitedly arrive for Memorial Day weekend, several with cases of beer and a visibly surly attitude toward men, gay or straight, even those of us who smile and say "hello." Many of the older lesbians in town lay low during this spring "invasion" too. I've been told by some that they feel invisible or dismissed by the boisterous, partying younger women and feel, as we do, that it's just not much fun to be around these particular gay people.

The men in leather land in Provincetown in September, strutting half-naked down Commercial Street in the evening, despite the cool temperatures, in their elaborate, studded ensembles. It looks like fun, but despite what I have been told about the gay leather community being warm and welcoming, one wouldn't guess that from looking at their faces. There frequently appears to be a conscious disregard for anyone not in their group's costume, even for those of us who, once again, are smiling and just saying "hello." Maybe looking angry *is* considered "sexy."

These experiences make Ray and me feel badly and a little disappointed. We feel badly for gay people who can't smile with joy at other gay people, and we feel disappointed that after all of the years we all have worked to create a world where gay people could easily find emotional health and happiness, significant numbers of our community appear to have missed the opportunity or have rejected the choice to be happy.

Ray and I are particularly heartsick when we see the impact that crystal meth and other "recreational" drugs have had on the lives of so many gay men, some of whom we know and love but can't spend time with anymore. We're losing some of our best and brightest souls to this highly-addictive, destructive substance. Why do we have this epidemic of debilitating chemical abuse? It feels like mass suicide to us. Some friends claim that such drugs make it possible for them to feel an intense sense of brotherhood with other gay men. It seems to us though that the drugs they're taking serve the sole purpose of helping them escape their very unhappy gay lives. How many of them would choose to take a pill that would make them straight, if such a pill existed?

We're equally depressed by the persistent problem gay men have with sexually transmitted infections (STI). It horrifies us to hear from gay doctor friends that some young gay men, called "bug catchers," actually *want* to be infected with HIV. Can anyone tell me what that's about, other than self-hate?

We read regularly in the newspaper with embarrassment and frustration that other gay men are so addicted to "getting it on" that they ignore common sense and all of the guidance they have been given on how to have safer sex. Young gay men always seem to be the group with the highest rates of infections. A straight black Seventh Day Adventist doctor colleague of mine, on the Surgeon General's sexual health task force, told me with bewilderment about his encounter with a man who reported having sex with twenty men the night before. He came to a clinic in Miami to see if he was HIV-positive. When he learned that his test results were negative, he announced that he was heading back out for more action. This preoccupation with sexual gratification, we feel, is an addiction, a sad indication of a very troubled soul, and most certainly not the greatest contribution we gay people have to make to our civilization. While HIV may not cause their death, as it did so many of our gay male friends in the 1980s and early 1990s, including our former roommate Patrick, getting infected on purpose or by foolishness is nevertheless a horrible, horrible waste of life.

It's not that I don't understand it all. As a walking-wounded gay man with an addictive personality and a need of affirmation and distraction, I know that I would have been fully capable of the exact same behaviors.

I would have loved, for instance, to have had a buffed body and, if I did, I would have wanted to promenade down Commercial Street, showing it off to have it appreciated.

I would have also loved to have had sex with lots of the hunky, near-naked men I saw on the streets and at the beach, and if they had offered me a drug that would have made our time together the most physically pleasurable moment of my life, I would really have wanted to take it.

If you got me into leather and I had found it enhanced my sexual experiences, as I suspect it might have, I would have played the sullen role too if I had thought it would have made me more appealing to my fantasy "daddy."

And I think I understand why the "baby dykes" don't smile and say "hello" to anyone other than to each other when they arrive in Provincetown in the spring. They're in the angry, separatist stage of their homosexual identity formation. I've had those feelings too, but there's a big difference in all of these examples between having the feelings and choosing to act on them.

It seems to Ray and to me, that finding and maintaining happiness in life as a gay, lesbian, bisexual, transgender or heterosexual person is really a matter of making choices that *enable* you to be happy. We all make (or don't make) such choices every day.

If Ray and I hadn't chosen to make a life of growth together in 1976, if I had stubbornly chosen to remain single, and had never chosen to enter a recovery program as an alcoholic, I'd probably be dead by now. Ray believes the same would be true for him. Choosing to be in our relationship, and choosing to be clean and sober, has kept us alive - physically, emotionally, and spiritually.

We're not a model couple, as some would have us be. We're two very flawed human beings who are working really hard to be in the world in a mutually creative, loving, and life-giving way. On a daily basis, we make hard choices that help make that possible.

If Ray dies before me, I sometimes worry what will become of me. In our relationship now, I draw the strength to make positive choices. If he dies, will I choose to start smoking grass and drinking again? Will I choose to wildly sow my oats? Will I choose to reconnect with estranged friends and family members out of fear and insecurity? I don't think so. I know better now. But, who knows?

Right now, we have each other's support, and we give each other encouragement to control our impulses to engage in behaviors we feel would create suffering in our lives and to make wise decisions that enable us to be in the world in a way that brings us both great happiness and peace – not every day and not every minute of the good days, but often enough that the hard work it takes and the tough choices we make to be so constantly and intimately in each other's lives are well worth the effort.

Maybe it's the effects of minor daily doses of Celexa and Wellbutrin, but, as I say, I'm very content with my life. I have enough of everything, and the wants are *not* for big pecs, or leather outfits, or multiple sexual encounters, or drug-induced ecstasy. I'm happy with the here and the now.

One of the most powerful influences on my life's joy is the spiritual guidance I have found in Buddhism and Taoism, and in the inspiration I get from the work of Joseph Campbell.

Buddhism teaches me that we each create our own suffering and that happiness is found in being present to the moment in all its possible manifestations. Taoism reminds me not to cling or be filled with wants, as they create discontent. Joseph Campbell teaches me that it is okay to let go of religious precepts as long as I don't abandon the spiritual path and continue to celebrate the many wonderful mysteries of life.

And more centering than the opiates of science and faith, I am prone to continue smiling even at people who won't smile back at me because of my safe haven in Ray. His love for me is very humbling. It anchors my every day and night. That's not to say I want to be with him at all times. He's no saint and there are lots of times that we both need our space. But we are soul mates, brothers in arms, and we're never far away from one another in thought.

One of the best things about the love we share, though, is that it is so liberating. The basic premise of our relationship is personal growth. For instance, if I wanted to go to the gym every day in the hopes of developing a body like the shirtless boys on the Fourth of July, Ray would encourage me to do so, never making me feel guilty for doing something stupid. But I don't feel the need to go to the gym because I exercise sufficiently for my health, I'm in love with a man who has always loved my body just the way it is, and I have finally come to the point in my life where I do too. I'm not trying to turn any heads with my physique, and that allows me to smile and laugh and be silly in public, whether or not that's considered "sexy."

If I wanted to wear leather and be put in a harness by a dungeon master, Ray would eagerly await the report of my adventure, but I know that if I found it very exciting, I would want to do it a lot. That's the way addicts think and behave, unless they're in recovery. And if I did it a lot, I wouldn't be home, holding hands with Ray as we watched television in bed. So, I make a choice.

And if I came home HIV-positive, or with another sexually transmitted infection, Ray would research them on the Internet to find out what challenges we faced.

The only thing I can think of that he wouldn't accommodate is if I started drinking again, or began taking recreational drugs. He would hate to end the relationship, but my addiction would threaten his sobriety, which is something he protects without compromise. He would make that very tough choice.

(For the record, I probably wouldn't be as understanding and accommodating if Ray came home in a leather outfit, with a boyfriend, or with HIV. There's a bit of a double standard in our house.)

My decision to live my life with Ray, as I have said, has made all of the difference in the quality of my life. And it *is* a decision. We all have wants -- occasional yearnings to act out in "wild and crazy" ways. No one is exempt from the fear of death and a life of mediocrity. Everyone has the desire to leave an indelible mark, to stand out as unique, to experience life at its fullest. But we also all make decisions. We feel our feelings but we must *choose* our behaviors. The choices we make determine the quality of our lives.

Our hope for gay, lesbian, bisexual, transgender, and other oppressed people throughout the world is that we all be free of the need to react to the pain and disappointments of our lives with self-destructive behaviors. We want all of those angry, tattooed, muscled and drug-dazed men, and all of those young brooding, separatist lesbians to remember themselves as sweet ten-year-olds who had dreams of living healthy, happy lives. There's always time to choose to be happy.

We've all felt the cruelty of the world in our lives, and our mothers could do nothing to protect us. Choosing as a gay person to take a pill to become heterosexual wouldn't change that. We're all walking wounded people, regardless of our orientation, gender identity, race, and economic or relational status. To enjoy the bodies, the time, and the lives we have, we needed to make choices that enhance our health and happiness. Perhaps the muscle boys, the leather men, and the young lesbians have found their health and happiness too, but if so, we wish they'd smile more, and maybe even wave back, just to let us know that they're okay.

7

The man who tried to sexually molest Ray when he was a teenager is now in prison. The man who sexually abused me as a child is dead. Both of those regrettable childhood experiences greatly impacted the amount of work we both needed to do to create and maintain an intimate relationship with another man.

The priest who wrestled Ray to the bed, tickling him, and seeking the joy of same-sex intimacy through such roughhouse foreplay, never succeeded in getting further with the wiry 17-year-old who was able to discreetly free himself of Father's hold and of much subsequent future sexual confusion. The priest got more satisfaction in his touching escapades with other boys with whom he was assigned to work. Ray saw the clergyman's name in the newspaper a couple of years ago when the country was in the midst of its hysteric response to "pedophile priests."

Besides losing trust in his sexual safety with clergy, and others in positions of authority, and freezing up when he received other unwanted sexual advances in the several years that followed, Ray came out of the experience pretty much unscathed. I, on the other hand, still have great difficulty being held from behind in bed, and have the same adverse reaction to the sight of shower seats as I do to the smell of turpentine. The latter was consumed by me at age 26 in an attempt to escape the sexual confusion, fear, and loneliness I felt then as a gay man. The shower seat was what I sat on to wash my father's back, butt, and genitals. He did the same for me. I was eight and he was 43. The practice, along with weekend naps during which I explored his body, and occasional camping trips when he would call me from the bed I shared with my brother Tom to come sleep with him, went on for four more years while I continued to feel enormous anxiety, arousal, shame, and ambivalence.

I made myself believe that everything about what we did was normal, except for the erections I would consistently get. Those embarrassed me. I didn't want my father to think I was homosexual.

Ironically, when I was in high school, my father called the mother of my best friend to share his fear that her son Henry and I were emotionally too close. It was not a healthy relationship for us, he said. Mrs. Grix hung up on him.

When I came out publicly in 1974, my father called an administrator of Marquette University, his alma mater and mine, and demanded to know what had happened to me in college to make me a homosexual. I hope they hung up on him too.

I couldn't hang up on my father. I sought my entire life to win his approval or our reconciliation, I'm not sure which. His desk drawer, when he died, was filled with letters from me that eloquently and earnestly sought understanding of our relationship. He was, for all practical purposes, my first lover, and we never spoke of it, ever, though mine were the only letters that he kept.

I didn't identify what happened between me and my father as molestation until I was exposed to the subject as a sex education trainee in my thirties. If a distinction can be made, I'd today say it was more sexual abuse, as Dad didn't *molest* me. He *abused* me. There was never semen spilled. I can't for the life of me remember if he ever had a complete erection. I think he did, but I'm not sure. Nothing happened anally or orally. It was all mutual touch, always accompanied by his phrase, "Go ahead and get it out of your system." Years later, I felt significant anxiety when I saw in the newspaper the exact same line quoted by victims of clergy sexual abuse. I also felt that anxiety when I saw the look on the face of my dog, Brit, who I, as his adult master, was leading into the shower to be bathed. He didn't want to go with me into that enclosed cubicle, and neither did I with my father when I was a youngster. And yet, I did want to go. The touch was intoxicating.

My dad abused me, I feel, by confusing me. He didn't allow me to have an adolescence that was free from the ambiguity I felt about sexual boundaries. I was a child. He was the parent. He should have stopped the showers as soon as he saw that I was sexually aroused. He never should have passively set up the nap scene, and he certainly should have let me sleep the night through in the bed I shared with my brother while on the road traveling.

But equally importantly, my father should have talked to me about what was transpiring between us. He should have given me a context for understanding it. Either at that time or later in life, he should have said, "I'm sorry, Brian. That was all inappropriate behavior on my part. I manipulated you and allowed you to feel that you were the aggressor. I withheld sexual satisfaction from you because I was ashamed and afraid. You're a good boy, son. Your feelings are natural and healthy. Some day I want you to experience the joy of sexual touch with someone your own age. If you are ever a father, please don't allow to happen with your son what I allowed and encouraged to happen with you."

Beyond revulsion for big bellies similar to that of my father, and for shower seats like that at the scene of the "crime," I grew up fearful of being trapped in situations I couldn't control and in great need of affirmation that I was physically of interest to my partners. I feel imprisoned today when I'm being held in bed by another man. And when I'm sexually aroused, I need to know that the other person is too. When they seem not to be, I'm back in bed with my father.

The first two men with whom I was sexual, after my fumbling experience as a college junior, were Catholic seminarians who were as sexually immature as me and who both created the impression of ambivalence about our sex, perhaps to deal with their own guilt. The ordeal of coping with their deceits felt consistent with my sexual encounters with Dad.

Later, when I was with Fr. Dan, he would on occasion announce after having sex with me that he was now going to go to a gay bar. Other times he would come to our bed with the smell of beer and the bar on him before he initiated sex with me. He toyed with my fear of infidelity.

Ed, the partner I aggressively sought after I broke up with Dan, didn't fall in love with me until I was tired of waiting for him to find me sexually desirable.

Ray was the first romantic interest who was clearly interested in me sexually, and his desire for me left nothing for me to crave. Instead of actually satisfying my need, the healthiness, goodness, and mutuality of our attraction ultimately bored me because there was no excitement in the compulsive search for rejection. For many, many years, Ray has had to deal with the legacy of my father's sexual abuse.

Another legacy of the abuse was the myriad feelings and actions that were required to cope with the secret about what transpired between my father and me, a secret that took me a long, long time to fully understand and to articulate. Even when I came out publicly and endured the expressions of humiliation my father shared with me about my public stance, I never dared make the connection between his behavior and mine.

My father didn't "make" me gay. I was having erotic thoughts of naked men long before my first shower with Dad. But, I always feared that if I mentioned my showers and naps with Dad, especially in my public presentations about homosexuality, everyone would immediately think that he made me a homosexual. I knew for certain he had nothing to do with it, but I didn't trust other people's abilities to make distinctions between "orientation" and "behavior."

Even now, in telling this story, I'm aware that some people may try to use the information about my abuse to discredit me or my message about the normalcy of homosexuality. But I can no longer protect the secret, as it is not only unhealthy for me to do so, but also because so many other men - gay, bisexual, and straight - have had similar experiences and need to be told that they did *nothing* wrong.

I have been through many stages in coming to terms with my sexual abuse. For several years, I denied it. When I finally acknowledged it as abuse, I said that it had no impact on me, and that my father was not to blame. Then I began to understand the extent of the impact it had on me, and started thinking of my father as a monster. Now, I accept that my father was not a monster but what he did was monstrous. He was a man who for whatever reason never learned to express his sexuality maturely. He may or may not have been abused as a child. It doesn't matter. Though it may explain his behavior, it doesn't excuse it.

During the fairly recent national hysteric uproar over child abuse, when everyone seemed to be recalling incidents in their childhoods when they were molested, when children in day care were grilled by police officers to build cases against their teachers, and when priests were being sent to prison where they were either murdered or put into protective custody, or were committing suicide from fear of what might be done to them, I knew that if I said anything about my childhood, my father might be arrested. I didn't want that to happen, as it would have served no purpose. He was in complete denial about the abuse, and I didn't want or need retribution.

Telling the secret today, long after his death and the deaths of his contemporaries, still fills me with dread, as I love and respect my father, and don't want others to think ill of him. In all other regards, he truly was a wonderful man and a good father. Yes, he was a conservative Republican, and yes he had trouble saying "I love you," and yes he would say dramatic things to get attention, and yes he could be a big baby, but he was an extremely generous, thoughtful, hardworking man who adored his wife, his children, and his grandchildren. I realize that my talking about my father's sexual behavior with me will hurt his surviving siblings, and his grandchildren who insist they would, as children, always prefer to be with Grandpa than anywhere else in the world, including Disneyworld.

But Dad's sexual behavior with me when I was a child is very relevant to the struggle that Ray and I have faced in creating and sustaining intimacy with each other as adult gay men. I don't see myself as a victim of my father. But our relationship was victimized by his inappropriate behaviors. Ray and I have worked hard to face the demons in our closets, to understand their impact upon us as individuals and as a couple, and to take the necessary steps to counteract the negative influences on our intimacy. So too, have a lot of other couples, gay and straight. Intimacy doesn't have a gender or an orientation.

I use the word "hysteric" to describe the national response to the childhood sexual abuse scandals because I feel that it has been way out of proportion to the crimes committed. The Boston priest convicted of pinching a boy's butt in a swimming pool died a horrendous death in prison at the hands of a person who beat the priest mercilessly in the wake of weeks of sensationalized press. The priest in question had done more than merely touch that one young man in the pool. He was an emotionally ill individual who victimized many, many young boys and forever scarred many of them spiritually and psychically. But he didn't deserve to be beaten to death. The murderer was the victim of childhood sexual abuse, but his passion was exacerbated by the media frenzy.

Pedophilia is the sexual abuse of children who are pre-pubescent. Ephebophilia is the sexual abuse of children who are post-pubescent, which means teenagers. Fondling a teenager is quite different than forced anal or oral sex on a three-year-old. But we, as a culture, haven't been making that distinction. We call it all pedophilia and we want every perpetrator behind bars for life. When they have served their sentence, we want them kept in jail forever, arguing that there is no cure, and that they always will pose a threat. If they ever do get out, we make it impossible for them to live anywhere but under a viaduct in a cardboard box. A person who kills another person with premeditation is treated with far less disgust and harshness, even when they kill a child.

Catholic and Protestant clergy have gotten the most press over childhood sexual abuse, primarily because of the trust that has been betrayed by people who hold an esteemed place in society. But parents molest their children in far greater numbers. It is estimated that one out of every four girls and one out of every seven boys in the United States has been inappropriately touched by an adult, generally one they know. The figures could be much higher in other parts of the world. Yet most of us don't want our parents or our parish priest in prison. We just wish the abuse had never happened because we're the ones who have to pay the price in our lifetime struggle for sexual health.

As a gay man raised Catholic, I would argue that I have been sexually abused far more effectively by Pope Benedict XVI, also known as Cardinal Joseph Ratzinger, than I ever was by my father, and that the impact of his carefully chosen, gratuitously hostile, erroneous, and dehumanizing words about my sexuality have left far deeper and more significant scars than the inappropriate touch engaged in by my father. I'd suggest that this is true for gay men and women throughout the world. But who would dare charge the Pope with the crime of sexual abuse?

If my father had molested my body rather than my brain, I'd probably feel differently about what punishment he deserved. But it would still be my responsibility to live my life not as a victim who could never experience intimacy, but rather as a walking wounded person who had every right to enjoy the full dimensions of love, and of true intimacy with another man, this one a person of my choosing.

8

The most important decision Ray and I each separately made after coming out and coming together was to stop drinking alcohol and stop smoking marijuana. Had we both not gotten sober and clean the relationship would have died and we might have too.

At the time he overdosed on pills, Ray was living and working in New York City, and I was coordinating the renovations of our home in Gloucester, MA, to which he commuted every weekend for over two years. I called his elderly landlord, Isadore Fromm, who graciously climbed to the third floor of his townhouse to see why Ray wasn't answering the telephone in his apartment.

"He's there, Brian, but he doesn't want to talk with you," the revered Gestalt therapist told me. "He's in pretty rough shape."

At Isadore's insistence, Ray came to the telephone and spoke in a low, emotionless voice. "What?"

"What's going on?" I asked. "I called you at work and they said you were home sick. I've been calling you all morning and you haven't picked up. Are you drinking?"

"Yes," he replied in a voice just above a whisper.

"And you're still taking the Antibuse?" I asked.

"Yes."

"That should make you throw up. Are you sick?"

"Yes."

"Will you please come home?" I pleaded. "Can you get yourself into a cab, go to the airport, and fly to Boston? I'll pick you up."

"No."

"Why not?"

"I don't want to," he replied.

After much begging from me and interceding by Isadore, Ray, who was humiliated and emotionally exhausted reluctantly agreed to come home. I waited in the car outside of the airport and spotted him walking oddly from the terminal.

"You're not still drunk. Why are you so woozy?" I asked after giving him a hug and kiss, and getting him strapped into his seat.

"I took pills," he said, and began to cry. "I can't take it anymore."

"We're going to the hospital," I said. "I want you to keep talking to me, Ray. Don't go to sleep."

After a harrowing drive to the hospital as Ray kept nodding off and I kept waking him up, I walked him into the emergency room where I filled out the necessary paperwork for his admittance. I followed as they rolled him to an area where they would pump his stomach. He called out for me in a panic when he couldn't see my face.

"Brian," he yelled, "where are you?"

"I need to be with him," I told the nurse who blocked my path.

"Are you related by blood?" she asked sternly.

"No," I answered truthfully. We weren't yet married, as this was in the mid-1980s and such a thing did not exist then for gay people in Massachusetts or anywhere else. And, if you said you were gay, most people assumed you also had AIDS. There was little training for private hospital personnel on homosexuality. Heterosexism in the medical profession was prevalent.

"I'm sorry," she said over Ray's persistent pleas for "Brian," "you can't go in. It's hospital rules. You have to be married or related by blood."

"He's my partner and I have power of attorney," I said with determination but anxiety that I may have just created a nightmare for my beloved. What kind of care would he receive after I left him for the night in this Seventh Day Adventist hospital?

"Call Betty Ford," Ray said after his stomach was pumped and he lay weakly in bed in the intensive care unit, holding my hand. "I want to quit drinking," he cried.

"You can go wherever you want to," I said, "But I think there's a place closer by."

I, too, cried most of the long drive back to Gloucester that night. I was totally exhausted, not just from the dramatic events of the evening, but from the months and months of relapses leading up to this night when I would worry sick about Ray, and agonize that if I was just clever enough, strong enough, and articulate enough, I could help him stop drinking. I needed Al Anon and didn't have the good sense to go. I was a classic co-dependent, enabling spouse.

The next day, Ray was admitted by our doctor to the hospital's rehab center. I drove him the short distance to the facility and waited with him until he got settled in. It wasn't the Betty Ford Clinic. It was cold, colorless, and there were no private rooms. The smoking room was filled with multiple-tattooed, tough-looking kids who were there because of their heroine addiction. Ray was a skinny, gay investment banker with Lehman Brothers, one of their best and brightest, and his muscular, straight bunkmates were blue collar teenagers hooked on crack. Without saying a word to each other, we both thought the same thing, "This is *not* the right place."

"It'll be fine. You'll be okay here," I assured him, as he physically shook with fear.

After he checked in and was given a pair of hospital slippers, I took his shoes to make sure he didn't run away.

I was very wrong about the Seventh Day Adventist hospital. The doctors and nurses were wonderful to Ray. And he and I were wrong about their rehab clinic. He *did* belong there. His three-week stay with them saved his life and profoundly changed our lives together.

My drinking was different than Ray's. He was an occasional binge drinker whose legs turned to rubber a moment after he looked sober. He had blackouts and alcohol-related horror stories. I, on the other hand, was a very controlled drinker – two glasses of wine a night, but every night, and I got to pick the glass. I never imagined that I was an alcoholic. When I drank too much, I got sick to my stomach, so I rarely allowed myself to go that far. I never had a blackout or any alcohol-related horror stories. (I'm a boring speaker at AA.) But, I really didn't need one to know that I relied way too heavily on alcohol to relax and to overcome my insecurities. I saw the freedom and peace that Ray now had in his life and I wanted to experience the same feelings.

It was six years after Ray chose sobriety for himself that I woke him up in the middle of the night to say "Honey, I think I'm an alcoholic." He had never suggested to me that I was, but he knew that I was making the first step in acknowledging that my life was no longer manageable. Eliminating alcohol from my life wasn't particularly difficult for me, but choosing to live clean and sober was one of the five most important things I have done for myself, physically and spiritually. The other four were coming out as gay, choosing to be with Ray, quitting smoking, and embracing a spiritual practice.

In many ways, choosing sobriety had as profound an impact on me as coming out and as embracing Buddhism as a philosophy of life. For me, sobriety wasn't so much about not drinking as it was about learning to be completely honest with myself and others, finding and affirming the truth in my life experiences, and taking life as it presented itself, a day at a time. My spiritual practice and my coming out experience have the exact same characteristics.

Recovering from addiction dramatically altered Ray's and my relationship, threatened its existence, and strengthened its core. When Ray embraced sobriety, he began taking full responsibility for himself, which left me without the job of taking care of him. I was panic-stricken.

Though he wasn't, as described by two protective friends, "fragile" when we got together, he had a vulnerability and a tentativeness about him that found refuge in my strength. This, of course, allowed me to feel needed, which made me love him all the more. When he came out of rehab, he didn't need me in the same way any more, and that not only frightened me but made each of us question the purpose of the relationship. What roles in each other's lives were we now supposed to play?

When I got into recovery, first from co-dependency through a program for Adult Children of Alcoholics, and then from alcohol and marijuana, through AA, I learned how to set boundaries for myself, which was both exciting and threatening to Ray. He wasn't used to me not seeking peace at any price. I began to stubbornly hold my ground.

It didn't happen overnight, or without a whole lot of therapy, long conversations, reading, reciting the "Serenity Prayer," attending meetings, confrontations, sleepless nights, and long walks, but the gears of our relationship, that had originally worked so smoothly, finally found their way back to alignment. The comfortable slippers of our pre-sobriety days were replaced by blister-inducing tight shoes of our post-recovery days, but eventually these, too, were broken in to feel cozy and of good use to us both.

We are very different people today than we were when we first came together, and our relationship is nothing like it once was. The romanticism about love, family, God, the Church, the country, the holidays, and the Democratic Party that we each brought with us when we first met has been enormously tempered by our experiences of ourselves, each other, and life as we have lived it. We're still romantics at heart – we continue to write mushy Valentines, adorn our home with family photos, acknowledge blessings before each meal, put out the flag on the Fourth of July, dye Easter Eggs, carve pumpkins, cook traditional side dishes at Thanksgiving, hang stockings at the fireplace at Christmas, cry at sad and happy books and films, and hope for another Pope John XXIII and another Camelot in the White House – but, as a result of our recovery, we're less emotionally attached to concepts.

Ray is now a very strong, independent (read "stubborn"), self-sufficient man who doesn't seek approval or support for his identity.

I am now far more capable of saying "no," freer from the need to make everyone happy, clearer about my wants, and more direct about my needs (read "controlling").

While much of this change in each of us, and in our relationship with each other, is due to aging and the expected maturing that comes with it, none of it would have been possible for either of us without choosing to embrace sobriety.

Today if we're going to overdose, it will be on dark chocolate, an addiction that apparently is considered good for us.

9

There are forty-three leather-bound photo albums in our bookcase which chronicle the life Ray and I have made or experienced together since May 4, 1976. From the beautiful woods of St. Joseph's Abbey, the Trappist monastery in Western Massachusetts where we would annually cut down our Christmas tree, to a remote village in Ghana where we enthusiastically joined the locals in festively flapping our elbows in a "chicken" dance, the photos capture two young men who are working hard but happily to find or create a safe place for their intimate love.

Jeremy, our Irish setter, now buried beneath a pine tree in Gloucester near the grave of our canary, Bing Crosby, appears in most of the activities of our first thirteen years. Brit, our yellow Lab, now buried beneath a pine tree in Provincetown, was with us for fifteen more. They appear in hundreds of photos.

There are shots of Ray and me, with Jeremy at our side, young and excited, stringing popcorn and cranberries as the primary ornaments of our earliest Christmas trees in Boston, and of Ray and me, with Brit at our feet, older and yet still excited, trying to find space for the hundreds of accumulated ornaments, each with its own story, for the on-line purchased fresh tree in Florida three decades later. In one album, we have hippy-length hair and big smiles as we're admiring pigs and sheep at the Deerfield Country Fair in New Hampshire, and in another our gray hair is cut stylishly short as we're swimming with sea lions in the Galapagos in Ecuador.

As we both love wildlife, there are abundant photos of them in the albums, a Noah's Ark of lions, giraffes, whales, elephants, cows, horses, zebras, penguins, seals, turkeys, leopards, mountain goats, bear, moose, elk, salmon, water buffalo, monkeys, and chipmunks, to name just a few. There are also many photos of architectural and natural wonders – ancient ruins, cathedrals, waterfalls, canyons, fishing shacks, forests, monuments, rivers, and gardens.

Mostly there are shots of friends – friends, friends, and more friends.

I have fantasies of sitting with these sacred keepsakes on my lap as I lie in bed in old age and prepare for death. I want the luxury of slowly recalling the people, places, and things which have so influenced our lives and given it such flavor. Doing so will remind me, as I try to remind myself each day, of how extraordinarily blessed I have been to have had such an amazing life companion, to have lived in such wonderful cities and homes, to have visited so many interesting places, to have "followed my bliss" in work, to have found a spiritual path that was so rewarding, and to have encountered so many remarkable people who have generously allowed us to share in their lives and accepted the invitation to participate in ours. I'm particularly grateful for the friends, gay and straight, male and female, with whom we have shared ourselves so intimately.

Our companions along the way have, for the most part, come and gone. Few faces which appeared regularly in the first assembled album are still in our lives today. Yet each plastic page holds the treasured images of people by whom we have been influenced and who we will never forget. They are grandparents, parents, siblings, aunts and uncles, cousins, visitors to our homes, business colleagues, neighbors, and former strangers we have met on our vacations.

There are photos of well-known actresses and actors, politicians, writers, network commentators and newscasters, children's book authors, civil rights personalities, sexuality educators, and priests and nuns, as well as far less publicly-known, but generally more dear to us, social workers, house painters, librarians, teachers, real estate agents, house cleaners, decorators, fishermen, lawyers, doctors, gardeners, retirees, and the unemployed, among others.

Our parents and grandparents are all dead, as are two older brothers, and many, many of our friends. The particulars of all of the settings have changed too, as nothing in life stays the same. Our renovated homes in Brookline, Gloucester, Atlanta, New York, San Francisco, and Naples have all been altered by new owners, Walden Pond is more trafficked, as is Machu Pichu, the Mariposa Hotel in Costa Rica now caters to heterosexuals, other vacation havens have closed, Detroit has deteriorated, Wichita has grown, and all else moves on.

Perusing these pages in bed in my old age will undoubtedly remind me of some of the lessons I have learned along the way. One, of course, is that everything changes. Another is to choose your friends wisely.

It's the advice I consistently give to gay men and women who write to me and say that they are just coming out. It's the advice I'd give to every heterosexual I know too. The people with whom we surround ourselves have a very powerful influence on the direction of our lives, most especially our physical and spiritual health.

Friends, I believe, should be sought or avoided on their ability to prompt healthy and continual growth. It is in rich soil that we seek to plant ourselves, not in toxic waste. Hope and cynicism are both contagious. Values rub off but not away. If we choose our traveling companions wisely, we'll enjoy life's beauty and joy, even when the sky is overcast. If we opt to hang out with "dementors," we'll complain that the sun is too bright or the smell of the rose is too strong.

Regrettably, many of us make friends with people because they like us. Not, who *are* like us, but rather who *like* us. All someone has had to do in the past is say that they loved one of my books and they were immediately endeared to me. That's not a good basis for friendship, but their faces nevertheless pop up in our photo albums.

Worse than that, I've also been attracted to people who *need* me. I'm a co-dependent magnet for anyone who feels weak, frightened, unhappy, or unloved. It's fun for me for awhile to respond with friendship because I feel so useful, but then they don't go away. And when I pull back, they get really angry with me. There are many photos of such people in the albums too.

Worse yet, is the mistake of making friends with people because you find them physically attractive. I have found that thinking with your genitals will always get you in trouble. I've been a "dick head" more than once and live with the embarrassment.

Trying to create long-term intimacy in a friendship that's just based upon people liking or needing you, or to whom you are attracted, is doomed to failure. Intimacy is most available to us with people with whom we feel equal, not economically, but emotionally and spiritually.

Many of us make friends with people with whom we share characteristics. Gay men, in general, hang out with gay men.

Lesbians frequently hang out with other lesbians. Transgender people hang out with other transgender people (but typically not transsexuals with cross-dressers). Conservative Republicans hang out with conservative Republicans.

When I'm in the cafeteria of any major corporation, I notice that most of the black people are sitting together, and most of the Asians are sitting together, and most of the Latinos are sitting together, and most of the heavyset people are sitting together. They're not close friends. They seem to just feel safer in each other's company. But does the relationship last outside of the workplace? Are they in each other's photo albums?

My single friends hang out with single people. Hanging out with couples makes them feel self-conscious. But are the single people they're hanging out with healthy? Do they drink too much or take recreational drugs? Are they racist, sexist, ageist, or classist? If so, what kind of influence do they have on the attitudes and behaviors of the other single people in their group?

If newly out single gay people fall in with a crowd of gay people who affirm themselves as healthy and normal, it impacts the self-esteem of the gay "newbie." If the crowd is closeted, self-deprecating out of internalized heterosexism, and self-conscious of what heterosexuals think of them, the gay newbie will follow suit.

If heterosexual men hang out with other heterosexual men who are homophobic, they'll find it hard to speak up and challenge the group when they start in on "fags." People who fear loss of status in a group are generally the most complicit in hate crimes and other forms of harassment. Thinking as individuals is most challenging in the Armed Forces, police departments, country clubs, circuit parties, and in fundamentalist churches.

Years ago, my best friend in eighth grade entered the seminary. While in high school and early college, he and his fellow liberal seminarians and I would sing with great emotion Simon and Garfunkel's haunting ballad, "Bridge Over Troubled Water." We looked at each other as we sang "when evening falls so hard, I will comfort you. I'm by your side, when darkness comes, and like a bridge over troubled water, I will lay me down." When I came out as gay a couple of years later, they all scattered in silence. The rejection of my former best friend was most painful for me at the time. "Hey, darkness has fallen. I've lost my job. I'm getting hate mail and threatening phone calls. I need comfort!"

We were all young, inexperienced, untested, and idealistic, so I understand now why the song lyrics were an ideal and not a plan of action. My heterosexual friend took his cues at the time from the frightened others, or they from him. He did come around years later after leaving the seminary to enter an interracial marriage that horrified and caused rejection by his liberal parents. We reconnected. People who have been beaten up by life hang out together too.

Emotional intimacy between friends, particularly between men, is a challenging thing. For me, intimacy is the heart of the watermelon, and worth the challenge of getting to it. It's the sweetest part of friendship. It's experienced as trust and is impossible without honesty. Many of us have flashes of it in our lives, like quick peeks or tiny tastes of something special. To maintain intimacy takes work, and sometimes lots and lots of work. And both sides have to participate in the work. Both sides have to share the goal of intimacy and be willing to sacrifice for it.

Ray and I are very intimate with each other, but we've worked really, really hard at it. We've struggled through over three decades of let downs, distancing endeavors, and stagnation in growth. We've had dozens of moments when we each were simultaneously thinking through which belongings we would take with us to our separate apartments. But we keep holding on, believing that the good we share far outweighs the challenges, and the lives we would have living apart from one another would pale by comparison to the joys we experience together.

We've lost to estrangement more than a few friends with whom we thought we had great intimacy, including family members. Some friends with whom we've shared many years and many experiences have drifted away after a struggle because the payoff for being close friends no longer outweighed the work that it required.

I miss all of the best friends who have moved in different directions. I don't begrudge them their journeys. Perhaps they found walking with us was not good for their health, physically or spiritually. Their photos which sit around the house and in our albums remind me of the good times we shared.

Gratefully, others have stepped in to take their space in our inner circles. Their pictures dominate the pages of the most recently compiled albums and are placed at eye level on the book shelves. We are wiser and more discriminating in our choices of friends than we were thirty-two years ago, and we are better friends to them because of the lessons we learned in our attempts to build and maintain friendships in the past.

We sadly acknowledge, that these faces too will pass, because all things change. Nothing stays the same, except that which appears in a photo album, and only when you keep buying more to fill.

10

On the occasion of a heterosexual friend's 60th birthday, Ray and I gave him a nicely framed picture of us on our 20th anniversary in Central Park. In it, I was behind Ray, holding him lovingly. Our heads were touching and we were both smiling happily. It was a beautiful shot, one we have given to our closest friends and family members. Our friend Jack thanked us with genuine enthusiasm, as did his wife Jean. He then handed it to the other two heterosexual couples who had just shared in the wonderful meal and delicious cake, and who were passing around cards and opened gifts for appreciation.

The next day, the two husbands who had been passed the photo, independently called Jack to say how unsettled they had found themselves feeling while looking at it. These were both very successful businessmen with whom we had shared more than one evening of dinner and board games in Jack and Jean's home, and who had engaged Ray often for his opinion on the stock market.

My feelings were hurt, as they unfortunately often are when I let down my guard with heterosexual men and women and then learn that they were not quite as comfortable as they had given us the impression of being. Like the time that Ray and I, during our tenth year together, were entertaining his folks at our cabin in New Hampshire and we asked his dad to say the grace before the noon meal. We all held hands, closed our eyes, and listened as Art solemnly gave thanks for the food, and then reminded God that it wasn't too late to send two good women into Ray's and my life so that we might get married and have children. But I get hurt less often and less deeply today than I did ten or twenty years ago because I'm much less invested in the acceptance by others, gay or straight.

Reflecting on that incident at the birthday party prompted me to wonder recently if my father would have displayed the same photo of Ray and me in an embrace on his executive desk in the Public Relations department of General Motors. Would Ray's father, despite his unrealized dreams for Ray, do the same in his Wichita real estate office, if he were alive and still working? Did their love of their sons ever embrace us fully for who we are, or was there any embarrassment with our intimacy, or shame that we weren't "real" men?

I often quote Lieutenant Colonel Oliver North, a radio talk show host and former principal of the Iran-Contra scandal, who warned during Bill Clinton's administration that if the President allowed openly gay people to serve in the military, "no *real* man would ever enlist again." Most members of my corporate audiences laugh at the lack of sophistication of North's observation, but my guess is that many of these same people would privately wonder about my relationship with Ray, as the vendors in Istanbul boldly asked us many, many years ago when we walked through the Grand Bazaar, "But, who's the wife?"

If two men are captured in an intimate pose, does it mean that one or both of them are "unmanly"? The very same photo of us in Central Park would draw little, if any, negative response from men in Italy, China, South Africa, or other countries where we have witnessed intimacy between all men as a common daily occurrence. Heterosexual men from India, in fact, have told me that one of the first lessons they needed to learn when they moved to the United States was not to hold the hand of their male friends in public, as it is seen in the U.S. as unmanly and an indication of homosexuality, which in America, they sensed, are the same.

That does not mean that men in these other countries are completely comfortable with homosexuality. Our tour guide in Cambodia, for instance, in response to my query about local attitudes toward gay people, told us that there are very few homosexuals in Cambodia. They're all in Thailand, due to the fertilizer they use in that country to generate three crops of mangoes annually. The homosexuals in Cambodia, he said, are transsexuals who want to be reincarnated as women in their next lives because it's easier in Cambodia to be a woman. (I decided that it was "a teachable moment" and we had a quick sex education lesson on our drive to

Angkor Wat.) But public displays of affection between heterosexual men in Cambodia are quite common.

If Ray's and my experiences, and those of most people with whom I've talked, are indicative of what's going on in the lives of many gay, lesbian, bisexual, and transgender people, what it means to be a "real" man, and what it means to be a "real" woman, are critical questions that must be addressed in the U.S., and around the world, if there is to be any serenity and integrity on our journeys. Perhaps this is true for heterosexual men and women too, but I think the stakes are much higher when you're "queer." (I hate and avoid using that word but it seemed to fit perfectly here.)

What makes a man a "real" man? And what makes a woman a "real" woman? I think that if we could all somehow agree on the answers to those questions, intimacy between same-sex people, regardless of their sexual orientation, wouldn't be so threatening, gay and straight children would not be bullied for failing to meet cultural standards of masculinity and femininity, transgender people would feel less conflicted as children by the breadth of their gender feelings, and fathers wouldn't have such a tough time putting romantic pictures of their sons and sons-in-law on their desks at work.

Ray says that he never questioned whether he was masculine enough. Lack of interest in sports was the only area that impacted his interactions with other Wall Street traders. As one of seven boys, it wasn't a problem for him because none of his brothers, or his father, played or showed interest in sports. As he wanted to be a priest, and priests aren't expected to be athletic, it just wasn't a burning issue in his life.

But would Oliver North say that men have to love sports to be "real" men? He may feel that real men aren't afraid of getting hurt, that they are driven by the desire to be Number One. One would only need to attend the International Gay Games to see how many gay men excel in sports. And it's my guess that there are a lot of straight men who fake an interest in sports in order to be able to communicate with other straight men, including their fathers.

How about going to war? Is that what makes a man a "real" man? When I filed as a conscientious objector to the war in Vietnam, my father was so angry and so ashamed of me that he yelled "I'm either going to rejoin the Navy or commit suicide." I lost a great deal of my father's respect then, and Oliver North might feel that it was correct for my father to be disgusted by my decision. He probably would conclude that my dad was the real man and I was the wimp.

I think that North and my father, because of their conservative political views, could have been friends. Both might have agreed that real men "kick ass," that they're not afraid of, or opposed to, killing other men. Real men enlist to fight in America's wars. And yet, some of their most idolized political heroes dodged the draft during the Vietnam War. Furthermore, it's my guess that there are lots of gay men who saw far more action in battle, and made far greater personal sacrifices for their country, than did Oliver North or my father, who was a photographer working with Edward Steichen.

Ray's parents wouldn't have been ashamed of me for being a conscientious objector. They opposed the Vietnam War and would have urged their sons to flee to Canada had any of them been drafted as I was. I wouldn't have been less a man to them, at least on that count. So, maybe fighting in a war doesn't make you a real man, at least not to everyone.

I've always liked being male. I never wanted to be a girl, but I did used to play with them – hopscotch, jacks, jump rope, and coloring and handwriting contests. I never dressed up like a girl, unless you count being an Altar Boy, and I was fairly good in sports, but not school-organized events. I was a fast runner until I started smoking. I was a fast swimmer and won races. I was often chosen early for pick-up games of basketball in someone's backyard. I could even throw a baseball really far. But I didn't *love* sports and playing them didn't make me feel macho. On the other hand, neither did my father or my older brother love sports, except when the Lions or Tigers were shown on Detroit television. So, maybe being good at or loving sports don't make you a real man either, except to some people.

In my relationship with Ray, we both think of ourselves as men in male roles, but if you really had to decide, based upon cultural stereotypes, who is the "husband" and who is the "wife" in our marriage, you'd pick me as the wife. I'm a good cook, I have an eye for decorating and landscape design, I do the grocery shopping, and I coordinate our social life – invitations, birthday, Christmas, sympathy, and Easter cards, "thank you" notes, etc. Do those skills make me less of a man? My folks were grateful for, and proud of, my nesting abilities. So maybe being good at things women are generally good at doesn't make you less of a man with everyone.

Is it simply my being a *homosexual* that makes me less of a "real" man?

The language used in most every culture to denigrate gay men suggests that homosexual men are considered less masculine than heterosexual men. There's "sissy," "fairy," "poof," "queen," and "he/she," among many other demeaning words. "Mariposa," the Spanish putdown for gay men, means "butterfly." But perhaps the selection of those words to describe gay men internationally is the result of the easy observation of effeminate gay men, who are much more readily spotted than are masculine gay men. And how many effeminate heterosexual men internationally have been assumed to be a "mariposa"? Sexist language about gay men makes it harder for most heterosexual men to feel comfortable in their masculinity too. No one wants to be thought of or spoken about as a "fag."

The word "faggot," spit with such disgust by some heterosexual men, communicates "You make me sick, sissy boy." Several years ago, two black men said it to me in Atlanta as I waited in the subway station to go to the airport. I was nattily dressed for a corporate presentation in suspenders. The incident made me self-conscious about my clothing and a bit frightened for my safety. Do clothes make the man? What then would Oliver North say about all of the muscled and tattooed gay men who wear jeans, flannel shirts, and work boots? Are they "real" men? They'd like us to think so.

In the adolescence of my gay identity, I was very uncomfortable around drag queens, cross dressers, Radical Fairies, and the Sisters of Perpetual Indulgence. All of them, because of their attire, brought up the fear that others would disqualify me as a real man because these other gay men were so "woman-like."

Even into the adulthood of my homosexual identity, I prided myself in defying stereotypes. I especially refused to do drag. Dressing up like a woman suggested you *wished* that you were a woman, I thought. It satisfies the heterosexual understanding of us. Thus, I resisted ever having my parents or older siblings see me in women's clothes, even on Halloween. Such was my strong fear of not being seen by them as a "real" man.

When I read in Don Clark's book *Living Gay* in 1979 his admonition that every gay man should have a dress in his closet, I was horrified. From my perspective, it was West Coast gay psycho-babble. What made it worse for me was that he's a highly-respected psychologist. If I met Don Clark today, I'd thank him, because today,

I have a dress in my closet. It's an orange, pink, black and white go-go shift. I also have a purple wig and a make-up bag. I got them all at a gay naturist event in the Poconos a few years ago when I was the canvas for a Drag 101 workshop. It changed my life forever.

There were undoubtedly many reasons for my emergence into a butterfly, each of which wore down my resistance to embracing my feminine side. Exposure to other gender-bending people, getting older, my spiritual practice of not clinging to anything including image, and the unconditional support I get from Ray were all part of the decision I made to volunteer to be cosmetically made-up for the nudist camp drag workshop. And once I climbed the enormous hurdle of my own homophobia, sexism, and heterosexism, I was never again the same Brian. I started becoming more of a real man, the *real* Brian.

I would be very pleased today to be made an honorary member of the Radical Fairies, the Sisters of Perpetual Indulgence, or the Renaissance Transgender Association. I don't care whether I'm thought of by heterosexual men as the "husband" or as the "wife" in my relationship with Ray. (I may even let Ray lead the next time we slow dance together.)

In the last few years, I've come to understand that I've been asking the wrong question. It's not what makes a person a "real" man or woman. It's what makes a man or woman a *real* person.

The terms "male" and "female" are biological designations based upon chromosomes, hormones, and genitalia. The terms "man" and "woman" and "masculine" and "feminine" are cultural constructs, as evidenced by the varying attitudes toward gender-appropriate behavior throughout the world and throughout time. They are subject to change.

I'm a slow learner. It takes me a long while to get my arms around change. Changing my focus on what it means to be a man or a woman, to be masculine or feminine, as I have said, has come from absorbing the lessons I see lived daily by the gay, lesbian, bisexual, and transgender people around me, particularly in Provincetown. The bearded lady, the drag queens (gay and straight) hawking their cabaret shows, the heterosexual cross-dressers (locally called "the Tall Ships") who make their pilgrimages to town, and the androgynous teens I see coming out in larger and larger numbers all tell me that gender expression is fluid. The boys who pump up and tattoo their arms in the same tribal wreath, and those lesbians who compulsively reject anything feminine also teach me lessons, such as: we create our own suffering by clinging to images of ourselves.

Heterosexual men like our friends Jack, who makes fun of himself as a scrawny Marine who never learned to swim, and Chip who kisses other men on the lips, and our nephew Michael who, at his wedding in the Hamptons to Christina, slow-danced with Ray, remind me of the courage of others to throw away privilege in order to feel free. Heterosexual women like my cousin Meredith who at five foot two inches tall stands up to and stares down bigger and more powerful men during political debates, and my Aunt Joan who finds no solace in dressing up in traditionally "feminine" clothes, also serve as incentives for me to let go of my cultural baggage.

And the example of living one's life as a *real* person comes to me most effectively from sharing a home and a dream with my spouse Ray. You'll not find a man, I think, who is more authentic. He doesn't care what anyone says or thinks about him, unless of course it's about a behavior of his that is causing them avoidable pain. Even then, he'll have to decide if changing his behavior for their sake will make him less real.

So, what is *real*? The best answer I have found comes to us from one children's toy to another.

"Does it mean having things that buzz inside you and a stick-out handle?" the Velveteen Rabbit asked the Skin Horse in Margery Williams' immortal tale.

"Real isn't how you are made," said the Skin Horse. "It's a thing that happens to you. When a child loves you for a long, long time, not just to play with, but REALLY loves you, then you become Real."

"Does it hurt?" asked the Rabbit?

"Sometimes," said the Skin Horse, for he was always truthful. "When you are Real you don't mind being hurt."

"Does it happen all at once, like being wound up," he asked, "or bit by bit?"

"It doesn't happen all at once," said the Skin Horse. "You become. It takes a long time. That's why it doesn't often happen to people who break easily, or have sharp edges, or who have to be carefully kept. Generally, by the time you are Real, most of your hair has been loved off, and your eyes drop out and you get loose in the joints and very shabby. But these things don't matter at all, because once you are Real you can't be ugly, except to people who don't understand."

The photograph of Ray and me, snuggling in love on our 20th anniversary in Central Park is Real beautiful. It's only unsettling to people who don't understand.

11

The valentine that I gave to Ray in the first year of our relationship was a spiral notebook filled with pictures cut out of magazines, accompanied by my biased recollections of our courtship.

The photos representing me, for instance, were of the very sexy Colt model, Al Parker. The photos selected to represent Ray were of the bumbling character portrayed consistently by Don Knotts. The sound of Ray's wonderful laughter as he paged through my labor of love is still making its way through space, assuring inhabitants of other planets of how happy gay couples on Earth can be.

When it came to representing my understanding of Ray's work in the field of finance, I had a picture of an old woman staring intently at her dozen Bingo cards, looking for all of the B-4s to dot with her dobber. Thirty years later, he tells people that this is still how I think of him on the job.

The truth be told, though I don't have much interest in matters of money, I do know that his years on Wall Street were a lot less fun for him than playing Bingo. Ray loved his work, as well as the people with whom he worked, clients and colleagues alike, but he *hated* the loneliness that he felt daily as a sensitive, politically liberal, gay man working in an office setting that was often the socially insensitive turf of boisterous, conservative, straight white "Alpha" men.

The coming together in our marriage of our very different career paths was fun for others to discuss, fascinating to observe, and very beneficial to me, as his income allowed me the freedom to do anything I wanted as a gay writer and educator without needing to make any money. But my work life made Ray's work life far more difficult than it would have been had he paired up with a man less on the cutting edge of the gay civil rights movement.

When we met, Ray had just left a job as a food and beverage cost controller for a hotel to take a "custodial" position at a bank. He laughs now at how he assumed he would be doing janitorial work but didn't care because he wanted the increase in pay to cover the cost of his night school college education. It turned out not to be sweeping floors but rather being a custodial accountant of mutual funds, a job which launched his lucrative career. Being very personable, a quick learner, and a hard worker, Ray excelled, became a favorite of clients, and was rapidly hired by a series of firms until he ended up at Lehman Brothers in their Boston office.

His boss at Lehman was a hard-drinking, foul-mouthed, bigger-than-life, short Italian with a heart of gold but little awareness of things gay. With him, and with many of Ray's trading floor colleagues, the word "fag" was a frequently employed synonym for "wimp."

Meanwhile, back in our apartment, I was coordinating Dignity's national social action initiatives, writing my column in the gay press, doing the layout of Detroit's gay newspaper, speaking on gay issues at colleges across the country, fielding calls day and night from gay people, sober and drunk, who needed to talk, and ultimately coordinating the City of Boston's response to the AIDS epidemic, and dealing with all other gay constituent needs for the internationally-respected Mayor, Kevin White, who hired me as his full-time liaison to the gay community, the first such position in the country.

Ray would wearily climb our three flights of stairs at the end of his day and enter the bustling center of gay activism in our living room. One day, he walked in on a meeting of local gay doctors and community organizers as we were writing the state's first "safe sex" brochure. At another time, we were drafting the Red Cross policy on blood donations. And one day, as he was walking past the line of two hundred people who stood waiting to get into the fundraiser we were hosting for our friend, the embattled Rep. Gerry Studds, one person said "Hey, no cuts," to which Ray smiled and explained "I live here." In every instance, Ray would peel off his suit coat, pull loose his tie, give me a kiss, and join in the discussion.

In some ways, this was a great gift to Ray. Coming home each night to a place where being gay was actively and enthusiastically celebrated nurtured his sense of self-determination and esteem. The phone calls, letters, film crews, reporters, strategy sessions, private consultations, and the dinner party conversations with the nation's leading gay thinkers that dominated our young lives accelerated his journey to self-love.

But how do you go from laughing at night with Elaine Noble, Tim McFeeley, Ginny Apuzzo, Sr. Jeannine Gramick, and Steve Endean to a Wall Street office the next morning where your identity is a secret? While Ray's excitement about his participation in the early days of the movement gave him a vision for his future, it also raised his expectations of life and made it harder to keep his mouth shut outside of the house, as so many of his gay and lesbian peers had learned to do twenty-five years ago.

And so, he came out, one of the first in the financial world to do so, initially to a handful of colleagues and then to his clients. For a short while, two of the major components of his life, his identity and his work, came together in a wholesome, happy way. Not only did it not matter to his clients, but they found his honesty refreshing, and became fiercely loyal to him, as he was to the firm.

Ray was then brought to New York to work in the corporate office and to run with the big dogs. Though he loved the challenge and the opportunity for further career advancement it provided him, he reluctantly slipped partially back into the closet and endured not only daily doses of verbal "fag" bashing, particularly by his new boss, but also an acute separation from me, who had stayed in Massachusetts, and from a safe space where gay pride permeated every room of our new home. Ray lived alone in an apartment Monday through Thursday and we talked at length on the phone every night. On Friday he would fly to Boston, and then drive an hour to our place in Gloucester, and for two days feel whole again. Those weekends were precious to us both.

Since coming out as gay in 1974 at the age of 26, I've never again had to endure the day-long horrors of the workplace closet. Initially poor as a church mouse on my own, I nevertheless have been free in a way most gay people, including the love of my life, have not been fortunate enough to be. My being gay, rather than being *tolerated* at work, was a necessary *credential* for me in writing, speaking, and serving in the Mayor's Office.

I suspect that the two-faced chaos of Ray's personal and professional identity, coupled with his spiritual hunger for honesty in his life, the high powered nature of his job, and his separation from me all contributed significantly to his hitting bottom with booze and his subsequent suicide attempt. During his recovery, and with his return to the Boston office, he came out without qualification and his work life became dramatically more tolerable. As a result, his client base grew in both size and stability.

After four more years in Boston, still enduring the "deep disappointment" and anger of a New York boss (the same one who said "fag" more often than "good morning,") because Ray hadn't come out to him sooner, Ray flew to New York to give notice that he planned to retire in a year. His boss there urged him to stay on and to take over Lehman's office in Atlanta. Ray said that he would but only if the firm affirmed his homosexuality by treating me as his spouse and paying my relocation expenses too.

We were in Atlanta for a couple of years. Our home in Ansley Park was the site of the office holiday party. That provided, perhaps for the first time in Wall Street history, the opportunity for the male spouse of the male office manager to guide the wives of the male staff through a tour of the master bedroom and respond to questions, at the same time offering decorating hints that could be incorporated in their own homes.

My speaking engagements, after having been dominated for many years by those on college campuses, were now primarily taking place in U.S. corporations, particularly for those in the high tech industry such as with Bellcore, Hewlett-Packard, Bell Labs, Lucent Technologies, and Motorola, and because of HIV, for drug companies, including Merck and DuPont.

By the time we moved to New York so that Ray could take over as Managing Director of Global Equity Sales, again at the request of his boss to delay retirement for two more years, Wall Street firms had emerged as my primary clients, starting with JP Morgan/Chase. Meanwhile, for Ray at work, the word "fag" continued to spice the boss's office conversations and conference calls.

My message to corporate executives is that to succeed in their goal of attracting and retaining the best and brightest employees, they need to create an environment where every person feels safe and valued. It's not enough to include "sexual orientation" in their non-discrimination policy, to offer domestic partner benefits, to have a gay, lesbian, bisexual, and transgender employee resource group, and to sponsor gay cultural events. The ability of people to feel safe and valued at work results from the "music" of the office, not the "words" of the corporate policy. How, I ask, do gay employees know for certain that they are valued? (*Not,* certainly, with the daily use of the word "fag.")

Ray became my example of how important it is to focus on the individual behavior of colleagues on a day-to-day basis in order to create a safe and productive environment. After years of stellar service as a revered boss and account manager, he walked away at age 45 from a significant salary because he didn't want to spend another day of his life feeling "tolerated." While no one at work was personally, openly hostile, Ray got tired of being the only one who wasn't asked on Monday about his weekend or on Friday about his holiday plans. His peers weren't conscious of the exclusion, and they meant no harm, but their strategy of avoidance created for their colleague an environment where he felt marginalized. And so, he gave notice, and in doing so, his frequent nightmares ended and he put away forever the armor he had reluctantly pulled on every morning for most of his working life.

That was a dozen years ago, and since then Ray and Lehman Brothers have changed dramatically. Ray looks younger, healthier, and far happier, and Lehman has become a leader in the financial world in its efforts to not just accommodate diversity but to *empower* it.

My professional career has gone from being fired for coming out as gay to now speaking to bankers in London, Hong Kong, Sidney, Singapore, and Tokyo about gay and transgender issues, at the same offices and to some of the same people Ray had managed in his career. A highlight of my work life was when I was invited to give my two hour presentation to the senior managers at Lehman's corporate headquarters in New York, with Ray in the auditorium.

Joe Gregory, the firm's terrific Chief Operations Officer (COO), and a colleague of Ray's, welcomed me and Ray, and spoke passionately to Ray's former peers and to those hired later, about Lehman's commitment to retain the best and brightest employees by creating an environment that *values* all diversity.

I've had some big challenges with speaking engagements before, like the time I spoke to 2,000 fraternity and sorority members in an outside venue at UCLA, but speaking at Lehman wasn't a big challenge at all. There was great enthusiasm in the room and great affection for Ray. It was a moment of bliss for us both. I've also had some tough audience members to contend with over the years, like the guy who sighed loudly, and dramatically looked at his watch the entire time I spoke because, he said, my message "would bring about the destruction of Western civilization." But everyone in the room at Lehman smiled and was clearly eager to learn.

Under the right circumstances, a speaker and an audience can do an incredible dance together, each following the other's lead, starting slowly but confidently, and building to a graceful series of turns that obliterate any awareness of time or outside distraction. We did such a dance together that day, and periodically, as the senior executives joined me in laughter at a humorous observation of our shared human experience, I would look over at Ray who was beaming and nodding with pride and gratitude.

At its conclusion, Joe stood to shake my hand, thank me, thank Ray, and thank his colleagues for their enthusiastic participation. "We've come a long way in a short time," he said, "and we have a long way to go."

Ray's old comrades surrounded him, patted his back, and handed him their business cards before we left for our hotel. I was scheduled to give a second talk the next day to a second group of senior traders, but Ray didn't feel the need to attend. "I got the closure I needed," he said, wrapping his arm around my shoulder as we walked down the street. "Thank you. You were just great. I was so proud."

In the many years that I've been working with investment banks worldwide, I've come to understand more about the game of Bingo they all play, but what makes a far bigger impression on me is how hard they all are trying now to create a work environment where people like me won't fear being fired and people like Ray won't need to retire.

So, now Al Parker, my Colt model alter ego, is walking up the stairs wearily after a long day of travel, and Don Knotts is home filling every room with gay pride. The reversed roles suit us both just fine.

12

When we flew to Ottawa from Provincetown with our dear friends, Tom and David, to get married in 2003, the Canadian customs agent asked our purpose of visiting her country.

"We're getting married," Ray and I replied in unison.

"Good for you," she said. "Congratulations."

It was a wonderful and unexpected start to an adventure of a lifetime. Our wedding in Ottawa, though quite simple, was deeply moving, and though there were only a handful of places in the world where the union would be recognized at that time, it felt remarkably significant.

Our decision to get married was casual. We knew that we didn't need the approval of the Church or the permission of the State to love one another as spouses. And we didn't feel the need to seek validation from a religious or secular authority for our 27 years together. Our desire for a "ritual" was satisfied on our 25th Anniversary when we drove to Vermont and had a civil union ceremony in the book-lined office of an 80-year-old Justice of the Peace. It is one of our favorite memories as a couple.

But when Canada sanctioned gay marriage, we decided to take advantage of the historic opportunity we were being afforded by our neighbors to the north. We both had worked long and hard for equality, and getting married in what could possibly have been a restricted time frame seemed not only the right thing but also the smart thing to do. Besides, civil unions, which were all that was available in the United States at the time, and only in Vermont, though very much-appreciated, nevertheless felt to us like "marriage-lite." Ray and I wanted to drink from the "Heterosexuals Only" water fountain. And if flying to Canada to quench our spiritual and political thirst was the only way to do so, then off to Canada we would go.

So, too, thought Tom Roberts and David McChesney. When we told them of our plans, these wonderful men -- with whom we shared a home lot in Florida, a passion for our West End neighborhood in Provincetown, and meals together at least three times a week, and with whom we have visited each other's birthplaces as well as several destinations around the world -- said that they, too, would like to formally acknowledge the fourteen years they had shared as partners.

Each couple paid the $125 fee, provided the necessary birth certificates, filled out the paperwork in City Hall, swore on the Bible to the truth of our responses, and signed as each other's witnesses the marriage licenses that were granted. The actual ceremony took place in the small but lovely gardens of a local Unitarian Church. We clipped blossoms from an overhanging tree for our boutonnières, and cried as we read our vows to the officiating minister, George Buchanan.

"We have gathered together to celebrate with you the marriages in which you are now to be united," George said in opening the ceremony. "Marriage is a natural relationship recognized by humankind from time immemorial, solemnized by the observances of religions and consecrated by the devoted souls in all ages who have brought its beauty to flower. It is not therefore to be entered into unadvisedly or lightly, but with deliberation and reverence."

Ray and I both promised "to have and to hold, for better, for worse, for richer, for poorer, in sickness or in health, in sorrow or in joy, to love and to cherish, as long as we both shall live." We had already proven ourselves to each other in that regard. They weren't untested promises. But saying the familiar words aloud to each other formalized our unspoken contract.

Instead of invoking the words of St. Paul to the Corinthians, we selected a reading from the *Tao te Ching,* and from *The Velveteen Rabbit.* The much-admired selection from the Tao said:

"Can you coax your mind from its wandering
and keep to the original oneness?
Can you let your body become
supple as a newborn child's?
Can you cleanse your inner vision
until you see nothing but the light?
Can you love people and lead them
without imposing your will?
Can you deal with the most vital matters
by letting events take their course?
Can you step back from your own mind
and thus understand all things?

Giving birth and nourishing,

having without possessing,

acting with no expectations,

leading and not trying to control;

this is the supreme virtue."

After lighting a center candle to symbolize the union of our lives, Ray and I, and Tom and David were told, "There are two of you, yet there is only one life before you. May this life be blessed and ever richer because of everything you bring to it as individuals." After signing the marriage registry and marriage license, and witnessing the latter for Tom and David, we were pronounced lawfully married and sent off with the words, "Ray and Brian, David and Tom, in a large sense you were married long before you came here today. In each couple you have been nurturing and building a loving relationship over many years. Today is the joyful confirmation of these relationships, the sharing of your commitments, wishes and hopes with these close friends. I thank you for sharing this very personal moment with us."

We then kissed, first Ray and me, and Tom and David, and then each other.

Before dinner that night, we exchanged wedding gifts. To our complete bewilderment and amusement, we had bought each other the exact same, allegedly very rare, antique bronze sculpted seagulls by the well-known Provincetown artist, William Boogar (1893 - 1958.) We laughed a long time about that, and marveled at its eeriness. They now serve to remind us in both homes of the wonderful trip we four gay men made to a foreign country together to have our relationships of love publicly acknowledged.

In reflection, what surprised me most about the wedding was what a powerful impression it made on me. I thought I'd glide through the ceremony and casually check it off my list as one more action I'd taken as a participant in the formation of the gay civil rights movement. Like many gay people I know, and I suspect most other minority members as well, I've built up a thick skin to not feel the pain from the arbitrary dismissal I generally get from those in power. Like the fox who couldn't quite reach the grapes in Aesop's Fable, I've pretended to believe that the full acceptance of the Church and the State would ultimately taste sour and not be worth the effort of securing. And yet, when I got such acceptance from the Government of Canada and from the Unitarian Church, there was a moment of surrender to the joy that can come from feeling unqualified affirmation.

But, I've learned not to let my guard down for very long, so after a quick cry and a prayer of thanksgiving, I dressed myself back up in my suit of armor for the flight home. When we entered the United States, where you are not allowed to approach the customs agent as a couple unless you are legally married, we each decided to avoid an airport security crisis by obeying the rules. But when asked what our business was in Canada, we each told the male officer, "To get married." He looked up at me, and then back at Ray, who had just been processed with the same address and with the same answer, smiled, and said, "Congratulations."

Sometimes the pain of rejection is self-inflicted.

We sent the photo of the four of us grinning in our suits and boutonnières to the *Provincetown Banner* and to the *Naples Daily News* newspapers. The former serves a very liberal community in Massachusetts. The latter serves a very conservative community in Florida where we lived at the time. Both newspapers, remarkably, ran the wedding picture and a story, as gay marriage in the U.S. was not yet a reality. The *Naples Daily News* even said they would begin running same-sex marriage announcements with those posted for heterosexual couples, as I had requested.

You won't know unless you ask.

The Vatican was less gracious in its response. In a statement entitled "Considerations Regarding Proposals to Give Legal Recognition to Unions between Homosexual Persons," it said, "Those who would move from tolerance to the legitimization of specific rights for cohabiting homosexual persons need to be reminded that the approval or legitimization of evil is something far different from the toleration of evil."

We're no longer shocked by the gratuitous hostility of the Vatican toward gay people. Nevertheless, reading that statement after our wedding felt like attending a funeral of a gay friend with Fred Phelps and his fellow Kansan Baptists holding a sign on the street that read "God Hates Fags." You have to breathe through it.

We didn't have a reception after the marriage in Canada. Friends had done so for us magnificently following our Vermont civil union, and we felt it was unnecessary. The dinner hosted for a small group of close friends by our dear friends Ann Maguire and Harriet Gordon in the Provincetown home after the ceremony in Vermont, and on the occasion of our 25th Anniversary, was memorable enough to cover both our civil union and our marriage. You see, Harriet cooked a meal for the occasion and Harriet does NOT cook. She boils water for the occasional lobster we bring up from our traps in the harbor, but the sign in her kitchen aptly proclaims, "What I make best for dinner is reservations."

The pork roast, over brown potatoes and carrots, pan gravy, and Caesar salad that this mother of two and grandmother of four so lovingly and nervously labored over all day were delicious and will never be forgotten. There was also a dark chocolate cake from the ever-popular Connie's Bakery that proclaimed "Congratulations, Brian and Ray."

The evening was spent around the table sharing stories of the historic trek to Vermont. The Justice of the Peace was a wise old man who had a rich history of writing, college presidency, and leadership of the Pennsylvania Federal Reserve. The movie made about his life included his experimental living in a cardboard box to better understand the plight of the homeless. He was a gentle, kind, and very supportive sage. At the end of the ceremony in his office, which was like the one I imagined occupied by Albus Dumbledore at Hogwarts, he asked us in lieu of a fee to make a contribution to the local community theater group, which was in desperate need of a new stage curtain.

Following the ceremony, Ray and I crossed the street to the gay guesthouse where we were staying, changed clothes in our room that was filled with flowers from friends, and then went antiquing, one of our favorite pastimes.

In the parking lot of the local group shop, a package-laden woman was getting into her car as we were getting out of ours.

"Are you guys brothers?" she asked.

"No, we're partners," we said. "And we just had our civil union."

"Well aren't you both lucky to have found someone as handsome as you both are," she said with a big smile.

Indeed we are. But better than handsome, we're lucky to have found someone as in love with the other as we both are.

13

If we had children, as I would like, Ray insists they would be in uniform, lined up according to age and height like the von Trapps, awaiting instructions from the blow of my whistle. I prefer the image of Auntie Mame taking them on exciting adventures and introducing them to new, magical experiences in order to stretch their minds. We have so much to give a child in terms of love and security. I often regret that we have not taken on that commitment.

But our experiences in our families of origin dramatically impacted our thoughts on having youngsters of our own. I wasn't ready to do so until recently when I got over my fear of our children dying. Growing up in a family in which you lose three of your six siblings and watching your parents repeatedly grieve those losses, colors your perception of what is involved in raising a family. Mom always said that a parent should never have to bury a child. I worried that it came with the role and I didn't want to face such loss.

Ray's experience of watching his youngest brother David, seven years his junior, uncomfortably answer questions from friends if Art and Mary were his grandparents, rather than his parents, set him against us having a child at our age. He feels that we're too old, and I don't disagree. If we adopted an infant now, I'd be in my late seventies when they were taking their first driver's test.

I wish that earlier in our lives we had been physically and emotionally more capable of having children, but we were both insufficiently available because of our work and aforementioned psychological roadblocks. And, it's not as if we haven't had children in our lives. Most of our beloved nieces and nephews on both sides of the family grew up with us as their pair of doting gay uncles. What limited time, because of geographic distance, that we had with them has *always* been very special for us, and I think for them too. They are a very big part of our logical family.

Likewise, for over thirty years, I have been involved in the lives of many young gay men and women who have contacted me through "snail" mail or e-mail seeking a welcoming ear, asking for advice, or just wanting to know that someone gay was there for them. With consistent affirmation of their worth, the promise that their lives could be full and happy, and the reminder that I would always be available, all of them matured quickly, and confidently flew off on their own. All but one, that is, and she was straight. "Lisa" was in my life for two very intense years. She became like a daughter to me, and our intimate relationship nearly ended mine with Ray.

I first heard from Lisa (not her real name) after she saw a PBS television program that featured me talking about growing up gay. She was sixteen. I reminded her of her dad, she wrote.

"I am not really sure why I am writing to you. The only reason I can think of is there really isn't anyone else to talk to.

"When I was a year old, my parents divorced. My mother got custody; my father got visitation rights. When I was two years old, my father picked me up for a visit and never brought me home again. I grew up thinking my mom was dead. That is what he always said.

94

In June (of last year) I learned the truth. I learned the truth and the next day he died. It wasn't unexpected but it still hurt.

"You are probably wondering what any of this has to do with you. If I tell you that my father died of AIDS and that he was gay, would it make more sense? I lived with my dad and Tony (his partner) ever since I can remember. It was the best, most loving, caring, supportive place in the world. They always said I could be absolutely anything and I could do whatever I set my mind to and I believed them. No matter what I did or said or felt, I knew I was loved.

"We moved a lot but mostly we lived in North Hollywood and San Francisco. It [homosexuality] isn't anything to hide or be ashamed of there, so growing up with gay parents seemed like the most natural thing in the world to me. I was never ashamed of my family. In fact, I was proud of them. As far as I was concerned they were the best parents a kid could have. Some people say that a gay couple shouldn't raise kids. I think they should keep their opinions to themselves. As far as what my preference was going to be concerning my life partner, my dad and I talked about it a lot. He always told me that the choice was mine. It was something that came from my heart and that no matter what my choice was, it would be fine with him and he would support me.

"My dad told me he was HIV positive when I was 10. I didn't really understand it all but I knew it was serious because of how they acted. Eventually, I found out how serious as I watched the one most important person in my life waste away to nothing. He died...on June 10...at 4:36 a.m. He died in my arms. I hadn't left the hospital in three weeks. The gay community I had grown up in took care of me. Someone was always at the hospital with Tony and me. They brought us food and clothes. They even cried with me on more than one occasion. This from people most of society says shouldn't raise children.

"My dad and Tony told me about my mom the day before he died. I was angry but I was afraid of him dying so I just told him I needed to walk and think. I think I walked every hall in the hospital before I finally went back to his room. I told him I loved him and nothing would ever change that. We cried and he fell asleep a few minutes later. He never woke up again.

"Tony and I talked after his funeral and he told me I could stay with him or he would help me find my mom. I thought about it for almost a week before I decided to find my mother. It was the biggest mistake of my life.

"I came to live with my mother and her husband in July (of last year). It was terrible from jump. Actually, 'terrible' doesn't describe it. 'Hell' is actually a better word. I went from a loving home to hell.

"August 1 … my stepfather beat me up and raped me. It was the first time but it certainly wasn't the last. It happened 3 or 4 times a week after that. I had been in Michigan for 10 days. I had no one to talk to. My mother had made it clear to me from the minute I stepped off the plane that she didn't want me here. She called me a 'dyke' and a 'lesbo' all the time. She said I couldn't be raised by 'fags' and 'queers' without becoming one. At first I didn't believe her, but after my stepfather started the night visits I started hating men. I am scared of all men now. I guess it kind of surprises me that I am writing to you. It's just that something about you reminded me of my dad. I guess that sounds crazy. Sorry.

"On May 20 … after 9 months of hell, I tried to kill myself. I ended up in an adolescent nut house. They kept me on a one-to-one suicide precaution for three weeks. I didn't talk for the whole time.

Finally, I broke. I told my doctor everything. They were talking about it [incest] in group and I ran out. Let me tell you a secret, when someone on a one-to-one suicide watch disappears alone, all hell breaks loose. I was hiding behind the door in the laundry room. They finally found me and they called my doctor. Sitting on the laundry room floor at the hospital, I finally told someone.

"I live with my grandparents now. I go to school and I go to church but I still don't talk. I still wish I had died. My stepfather is in jail and my mom doesn't want to see me. She says I have ruined her life. The court wouldn't let me go home to Tony but he was at the trial every day. My mom never came. I am not allowed to tell people about my dad being gay or having AIDS. When people ask how he died, my grandparents tell them cancer. My daddy taught me not to lie so it is just easier not to talk.

"I don't know for sure why I am writing to you. I admire you for what you do. I hope and pray no one has to be made to feel ashamed anymore. I used to know who I was, what I wanted, how I felt and I cherished life but not anymore. Please keep telling people because their not knowing hurts everyone.

"I am starting to cry and I can't let myself, so I will go now. Thanks for listening."

I was, of course, deeply moved by Lisa's story and immediately responded with a strong letter of support and encouragement. She responded right away with a telephone call and we subsequently talked for an hour nearly every day of the week for two years. Ray, who was also compelled to compassion by her letter, encouraged me in my role of mentor.

I looked forward to Lisa's calls and to her letters. Eventually, she shared with me photographs of herself, of Tony and her dad, of her grandparents, and of her cousin, Anna, whom I later learned was a tough-talking, no-nonsense woman who hated her weight.

Anna called me one day and confirmed all of the details in Lisa's letter, told me that she, herself, had a difficult time understanding and accepting homosexuality, and knew that it must be hard for Lisa to now be in a Baptist household where she was forbidden from discussing her life with her father and Tony.

Sensing she could use some help in explaining homosexuality to her new family, I sent Lisa copies of my books and the two videos that she had seen of me on television. Though I was initially cautious about getting too involved, I enjoyed feeling that I was helping this young woman. Lisa was a very bright, exceedingly pleasant and enormously gifted young woman, wise beyond her years. Her life, though, continued to be a nightmare of heartbreaking drama.

When she first called me, I initially just listened because what Lisa most needed was to feel understood. Often she would ask me "Brian, when will it stop hurting?" I encouraged her to talk to me about her life with her father and Tony, to stay in therapy, and to have patience with her cousin and her grandparents.

With her permission, I shared with Ray the basic content of our daily conversations. He continued to encourage me in my support of Lisa, but knowing my propensity for needing to be needed, and my subsequent inability to set boundaries, he repeatedly cautioned me about getting too personally involved. Privately, I dismissed his advice, feeling that he was too cerebral in his thinking, that his 12-Step Program was making him too emotionally detached from others, and that just maybe he was a little jealous of the attention I was giving to Lisa and not to him. Besides, my involvement in Lisa's life was making an enormous difference. Her grandparents read my books, watched my videos, and subsequently re-hung the photo of their son in their home. Grandma confronted her minister with his homophobia and Grandpa surprised Lisa by dressing up as Santa at the Christmas party that she had helped host for children with AIDS.

When Lisa graduated from high school, she had the highest grades in her class and was asked to give the valedictory address. In it, she credited me with saving her life. I was deeply moved and sent her a dozen roses for the occasion.

I never felt Ray's love for me wane because of Lisa's and my mutual adoption, but his reservations about my unquestioning involvement in her life increased in number and in volume, as did his frustration that I wasn't listening to his caution. But Lisa's need for help was getting more and more acute, and I couldn't abandon her.

The first crisis came when Tony succumbed to AIDS. Lisa was inconsolable for weeks. Then, Grandpa had a stroke and after lingering for weeks, he too died. Grandma carried on and became a strong unflinching advocate for Lisa, but then one morning, she found a small lump on her breast while showering, was diagnosed with cancer, and after a heroic battle, she too died. We grieved together for a month, and then Lisa's homophobic mother demanded that she come home and live with her. I thought about asking Ray if she could come live with us, but didn't.

My own father died in the midst of all of this and Anna came to his funeral in Detroit. Lisa was very upset that she couldn't be there, but had to be away for a college-related event. We had yet to meet in person, which we both lamented. Ray and I talked with Anna at length during the wake. She thanked us for being so good to Lisa. Anna was short and heavyset as she had appeared in the photograph, and had a sweet smile. She was very grateful for the big hug and kiss that I gave her before she left the mortuary.

Weeks and months passed and Lisa and I, despite our efforts, had yet to meet face to face, which made Ray increasingly suspicious. "Each time that you're scheduled to meet, something comes up for her. Don't you think that's strange?"

What I thought was strange was his questioning the truthfulness of a young woman who was so sweet, so in need of my help, and who meant so much to me.

"But don't you think she and Anna sound a lot alike on the phone?" he asked.

What I thought was that he was trying to ruin my relationship with Lisa. "Why don't you get on the phone the next time she calls and listen in," I suggested. "We'll get Anna on the phone too and you decide for yourself." He did so and felt that though they sounded alike, there was enough difference to cast doubts on his theory. But he was still suspicious, and we began to experience real tension in our relationship. I felt I was being forced to choose between my spouse and my "daughter." I hated the feeling and resented him for creating the conflict.

Lisa soon called to say that she had just learned that Anna's younger brother was gay, and would I be willing to talk with him. "Of course," I said. "Tell him that I'm here for him."

Shortly thereafter, Anna's younger brother was gay-bashed and seriously hurt. I immediately called the Triangle Foundation in Detroit, an organization whose focus is anti-gay violence, and reported the crime. They had no record of it but promised to call the local police and follow up.

All of our friends knew about Lisa, Anna, Grandma, Grandpa, Tony, and the gay brother. I worked the story of Lisa into my speeches as an example of a brave straight soul who was fighting homophobia in her own family. I wrote a long chapter about her for my book *Now That I'm Out, What Do I Do?*

Ray remained skeptical and urged me to question her on why we hadn't yet met, why the Triangle Foundation wasn't able to verify the gay-bashing of her cousin, and why she hadn't yet signed the release form for the book chapter I had written. I continued to resent his doubt, but at the same time I was horrified by the possibility that my little girl, my wonderful young friend whose life I had so positively impacted, could possibly have lied to me about *anything*, even once. Reluctantly, I called an attorney friend in Detroit who agreed to have his firm's private detective verify the information that I gave him.

"Brian," he said in a call a few days later, "there *is* a 'Lisa Reynolds' at the address you gave us, but I regret to say that she's not 18 as she told you, she's 28, and there's no record of an 'Anna' at that address or anywhere else in the area."

I was stunned and devastated. In an emotional state of panic, I immediately called Ray to tell him that he was right. He kindly did not say "I told you so." Instead he said "I'm really sorry, Brian. I know how terribly hurt you must be."

Next I called my publisher and said "Please pull the chapter on Lisa. Her whole story is apparently a lie."

It took me a long, long time to get over the deception. Lisa called me once more to ask why she hadn't heard from me recently and would I still be willing to counsel her gay cousin. I gently backed out of the relationship, at the advice of psychiatrist friends, and said that I was unable to invest the time that would be needed.

Ray nurtured the wound that I didn't trust his judgment; that I had pigheadedly pursued the relationship with Lisa because of my co-dependency. My need to be needed had taken precedence over our relationship and our commitment to the problem-solving practice of honest talking and listening that he and I had created to guide us through tough times.

My ability to trust others was decimated. I became suspicious of every call, letter, and e-mail that asked for help. At the same time, I hoped in vain that my lawyer friend would call and say, "I'm sorry, Brian, we were wrong. She's exactly who she says she is. Lisa and Anna are not the same person. The woman who came to your father's funeral was not a fraud."

He never called though, and a few months later, Ray came home with a copy of a national magazine that had a story that sounded exactly like my experience. "You need to read this," he said. A woman by the same name as the one given to me, using all of the other names she had used in her tale of woe to me, had duped Armistead Maupin, the celebrated gay author of the *Tales of the City* series, with a completely different story, and had profoundly impacted his relationship with his partner, Terry Anderson. I knew Armistead, so I wrote and told him what had happened to me. I also sent him copies of the photographs Lisa had sent to me. "Looks like our girl," he replied confidently.

Over a period of time, in person and on the phone, he and I shared stories and feelings. We both felt emotionally spent. "She did the same thing to Paul Monette as he was dying," Armistead said. "What's her thing with gay writers?"

20/20, the network news program, got into the act, and tried to make the connection between the two Lisa's who had scammed us. The show's producer had me listen in as she interviewed by phone the woman who had called me for two years. When Lisa/Anna hung up, I confirmed that it was "Lisa," but speaking in "Anna's" less sweet voice. The producer then told me that she was having trouble proving that Armistead's Lisa and my Lisa were the same person, but that in a prior interview, the young woman who had become my "child" explained that she had multiple personalities.

It's been several years since all of that transpired. Armistead and Terry broke up and Armistead wrote *The Night Listener* as a form of healing. Ray has forgiven me for not trusting him, though residual anger sometimes works its way into our disagreements on other issues. I have regained my trust in strangers, though I generally no longer carry on long-term communication with them. And I have forgiven Lisa/Anna, or whoever she is. I don't think she had multiple personalities; usually they don't pass the phone back and forth between themselves, and I don't know what motivated her to contact me. But she never asked for anything other than my time and attention, which I gave to her willingly. Though I still wish her story had been true, I don't wish that she hadn't written, as I learned many valuable lessons about myself which have made me a much healthier person.

I have better boundaries today than I did then, and better judgment. I still think I'd be a good father, though I know that I'd want to parent a child as a member of the Brian and Ray team. I need Ray's rational thinking to balance my own. We keep each other honest.

Though we won't adopt and raise a child of our own, I look forward to having great-nieces and great-nephews to spoil, to introduce to other sections of life's great menu, to share the joy and insights of my journey with Ray, and perhaps, occasionally, with great restraint, to get their attention by blowing a whistle.

I also look forward to continuing to receive the mail that comes from gay people, young and old, who need an ear, a little advice, and to know that they're not alone. *That* I can do.

14

We have never argued over money. That doesn't mean we've never argued. Hell for both of us would be spending eternity with me driving and Ray riding as the passenger. Or, worse yet, it would be us carrying something together that we couldn't carry alone, such as a long table or a ladder.

"What's that face about?" I'd ask.

"You started before I was ready. Now what's that face about?"

"You sound like your father."

"You sound like your grandmother."

"You're too bossy."

"You're too sensitive."

Where was I? Oh yes, not in Hell. I was talking about money.

Not once in over thirty years has it been an issue of conflict between us, which is quite amazing because Ray is a conservative saver, and I have no sense of or interest in personal finance. That doesn't mean that we haven't individually felt stress over finances, but we haven't imposed our anxiety on each other.

When we first met, I didn't have a credit card. I always paid cash with what little cash I had. Ray said that I needed a card to establish credit, so in a year, I had thirty. Every time I shopped and the clerk asked me if I'd like to open an account with the store, I'd say "yes." No one had more credit cards than me, but I was only doing what I was told. When my wallet got bigger than my pant's pocket, Ray cut all of them up, except for an American Express and a Visa card. "That's all you'll need," he assured me.

I don't consciously disdain economics, but my eyes glaze over when Ray starts talking about "the Fed" raising lending rates, and I never read the business section of the newspaper unless there's an article about one of my clients, and then I do so hoping it's about their diversity initiatives and not about their acquisitions or losses. This I readily admit to them when I begin addressing their senior executives. I couldn't fake financial acumen if I wanted to.

In my mind, if I'm shopping and I don't buy something I like that is valued at $1,000, I now have $1,000 that I'm free to spend. If I get the coveted object for $750, I now have $250 to spend on something else. Ray shakes his head with amusement.

I grew up in a house where money wasn't an issue. We didn't talk about it. We weren't rich, but in looking back I realize we were more comfortable and secure than most of my peers. Dad would occasionally call all of his children together to discuss a large phone bill, but we never felt it was a serious conversation. We would end up making him laugh by blaming all of the calls on Maureen, the youngest, who couldn't dial a phone at the time.

Dad communicated his love through money. Instead of saying "I'm sorry," or "I'll miss you," he would stuff a couple of twenty dollar bills or more into our pockets and say "Buy yourself something." If one of us had an automobile accident, he never talked about how much it would cost to repair the car. He always said, "As long as you're all right, your mother and I are happy."

Mom was a bit more "frugal" than Dad. I always suspected that people who came to the house to sell things like Girl Scout cookies said a prayer that my father, not my mother, would answer the door. She'd buy a box or two. He'd take a case to support the cause. Mom was generous with her time and attention, and our friends were always welcome to stay for dinner or the night, but it was Dad with whom you'd want to go shopping.

Ray didn't grow up poor, but with far less financial security than me. Money was a very important topic of conversation in his house, and it created a great deal of tension between his folks and among his siblings. When Ray's father had the "nervous breakdown" and his mother immediately moved the family into a smaller house, Ray learned at an early age of the power of money to create or destroy security. His mom and dad were not cheap, but they watched every penny. They had to. For the two years that his dad was in the hospital and at home recovering, the family lived off of savings. Ray felt embarrassment about the family's plight, and anxious every time the subject of money came up.

Unlike me, Ray paid for his college education. And unlike me, he had to buy his first car. He never borrowed money from his parents, which is something he is still very proud of today. Being financially secure for him, even at an early age, became synonymous with freedom. He judged his manhood by his ability to provide, initially for himself, and then for both of us and our future.

My folks both openly admired Ray's work ethic. He started in his early teens bagging groceries and mowing lawns, and never stopped. My mom bragged to others about how he had walked many miles to work through several feet of snow during the blizzard of 1978 in Boston, and was the only one in the office for most of the morning. Ray felt driven to succeed. Unbeknownst to me, he privately fretted about how much money would be enough to guarantee our lack of dependence upon others. He never wanted again to experience the financial insecurity that dominated his childhood.

Yet, Ray has never told me, "We can't buy that." Even in the beginning of the relationship, when we made $10,000 a year between us, money was never raised as a concern. Lucky for him that I've never been interested in clothes, jewelry, electronic gadgets, fancy meals or hotels, exotic vacations, or automobiles. He has much more expensive tastes than me, but I have always trusted that he wouldn't spend what we didn't have. He has hoped the same was true of me.

From the first year of our relationship, Ray and I have had a joint bank account. Our wills name the other as the sole beneficiary of our estates. Though we didn't formalize it with a document, we have always agreed that if we broke up, we would divide our wealth in half. What was mine was his and vice versa.

I was comfortable with that understanding in the beginning, because we made about the same amount of money and we had accumulated very few things. He had some furniture. I had a car. When Ray began making significantly more money than me, he assured me that it wasn't an issue for him, and that his success wouldn't be happening if he wasn't in relationship with me. I created home, he said. His income enabled me to do it. In his mind, the quality of our lives was the result of our team effort.

But I struggled for many years with feelings of inadequacy about not carrying my weight. In the beginning it was easier, as we didn't spend much. I facetiously made the case for how I was financing our vacation with the $20 that I was paid every month by each of the seven gay newspapers which published my monthly column. We laughed about how that same $140 had also been cited as the source of revenue for our groceries, birthday gifts, rent, and doctor's bills.

When we started spending much more money to buy and furnish a home, and then a cottage, I became frustrated that all of the work I put into managing the renovations of the house, and its weekly upkeep was not valued sufficiently. But it wasn't Ray who didn't value it, it was me. He was very happy to come home to a clean house, healthy pets, good food, and paid bills. But just as he was measuring his manhood by what he made in salary, so too was I assessing my value by the money I was or wasn't contributing to our bank account.

With time, my career as an educator on gay issues began to take off. I didn't make a lot of money with my books, videos, and talks, especially compared to Ray's Wall Street salary and bonus, but it was respectable. Funny thing though, the more work I got, the less Ray liked it, not because he begrudged me the success, but because the money didn't compensate for the household burdens that he now was forced to share. "Can you pick the dog up at the kennel on your way back from the airport, honey?" I'd ask. "I don't get home until tomorrow. I left a meal for you in the freezer."

Ray's retirement a dozen years ago once again altered our financial picture. After many years of working very hard at jobs in which he endured the loneliness of being gay, he had made enough money that, to his calculations, would carry us securely into old age. When the cost of renovations on a home we bought in San Francisco was double what was estimated, he suddenly felt the same insecurity he endured as a child. "We don't have enough money!" Yet, he never imposed those feelings on me. I continued to get busier and busier with my work, making several times more for one corporate presentation than I did for writing a year of columns. Again, my income was nothing compared to what Ray had brought in, and continued to make with his investments, but it satisfied my need to justify my fiscal contribution to the relationship. And now, what I make really does finance our vacations and a few other things as well.

Ironically, in the first few years of his retirement during which Ray took over many of my household tasks, he had to struggle a bit with whether *his* contribution to the relationship was being adequately valued. As was true with me, this angst was self-inflicted, tied into ego and to the culture's concept of manhood. In his wisdom, he let go of it.

Ray being one of the most generous and thoughtful people I've ever met is undoubtedly the reason why money hasn't come up as an issue with us. I would never have experienced the quality of life that I have today had he not shared equally the fruit of his labors. He continues to insist the same is true for him. Had we not been partners in life, he says, he possibly would have made the same amount of money but not enjoyed it nearly as much.

We're very lucky, I think. Money seems to be an enormous issue of stress in many relationships that we've seen, both gay and straight. Sometimes when we're out with another long-term couple, we'll watch with bewilderment as they negotiate their individual shares of the meal. It's as if they're roommates and if they don't do the financial accounting at that moment, they'll forget and screw up the arrangement.

Despite the disparity in our incomes, Ray has always let me be the one to pull out the credit card to pay for the meal, even when our guests were his parents, siblings, or nephews. When we're with our friends Tom and David, one person from each couple puts down a credit card and we ask the server to divide the bill in half. With some other people, though, money is collected according to what each person ate or drank. The only time we appreciate this prolonged negotiation is when the others have consumed a lot of expensive alcohol.

These same couples, who figure out their individual shares, have told us that their finances are also divided. They have a joint household account, but their money is otherwise separate, and their wills bequeath some of their estates to others. We even know of a couple with one partner who is very wealthy because of his line of work, and the other partner, because of his different kind of work, is not. The "City Mouse," as I like to call him, owns lots of property which is enjoyed by the "Country Mouse," but only until the wealthier of the two dies. Then, all of the estate goes to an estranged family.

I know there are multiple reasons why couples work out economic agreements different than ours. One might have inherited significant wealth that is considered "family" money. Great-great-grandfather Clarence, for instance, bought the land and it has been in the family ever since. Family heirlooms are another concern. Great-grandma's portrait was painted by John Singer Sargent and blood would be shed if it was left to the lesbian "roommate."

Maybe the couple decides that separate accounts are necessary because one of the two is a compulsive gambler or just irresponsible with money. Maybe keeping things separate helps both people feel as if they could leave the relationship easily, and such a sense of freedom is necessary for them to stay together.

None of that would have worked for Ray and me. Our arrangement might not work for them either. But I'm glad that it was Ray who climbed into my car back in Boston in 1976. Had it been one of them, it could have been Hell for me. Maybe not as bad as lifting furniture with Ray for eternity, but much less happy and secure than the life he and I have built together in the here and now as equal partners.

15

Sadly, some gay men believe that a man isn't really *gay* unless he has had anal sex. That's utter nonsense. It's as misinformed as believing that if people don't masturbate there is something wrong with them. Not only is it immature thinking, but they are both sexually unhealthy positions to take.

There's nothing wrong with anal sex. Many men, straight and gay, enjoy it very much. But you don't have to like it to be a gay male and it doesn't make a "man" out of you to engage in it.

The most satisfying sexual experiences, I find, are those which are freely and fully sanctioned by the individual or individuals involved, give pleasure, and communicate positive feelings. For Ray and his neighborhood friend, it began in early childhood when they experimented with genital touching by "playing doctor" at age five. For me today, as for many people my age, it's masturbation, or "*self*-pleasuring."

Having sex can be very healthy and lots of fun, whether it's with yourself or with others. I suspect that if more Catholic priests, fundamentalist ministers, conservative Republican congressmen, and other champions of "family values" were taught how to self-pleasure without guilt, they wouldn't be as prone to end up in newspaper headlines for inappropriately acting out with others. Such sex is *not* healthy.

To be sexually healthy people, we have to *love* our bodies, our genders, and our orientations, and not disparage other people for being different. We need to choose freely and responsibly the activities in which we wish to participate, and not put down the choices of others, if those choices are free and responsible. That's why it's immature and sexually unhealthy to make statements such as "*real* gay men need to have anal sex." Many gay men don't, and some who do don't enjoy it but won't admit it.

That's neither here nor there to me. Other gay men have to figure it out on their own. At one time in my life, I had anal sex and enjoyed it. Now, I don't. What you like doing sexually in life, and how often you want to do it, changes with time, as is true with most things.

What makes me sad and sorry, though, is the destructive false messages about sex that are imposed on gay men and lesbian women who are just beginning to explore their sexuality. They get a list of sexual "dos" and "don'ts" before they get a chance to determine for themselves what satisfies them and makes them happy.

They don't get such false messages from reading *The Joy of Gay (*or *Lesbian) Sex.* Rather, they hear them passed on, like urban legends, on bar stools and in porn flicks, in romance novels and in their national and local gay periodicals. The uninitiated and the sexually shy listen or read quietly and make mental notes. Then those silly pronouncements about gay sex end up in e-mails to me from frightened men who say "I'm attracted to men but I don't think I'm gay because I don't want to have anal sex."

There was a bisexual former porn star in Provincetown recently who was featured in what I assume was a talent show. Considered a "sex god" by some, his name and prodigious penis are well-known to many gay men. Plastic dolls have even been created in his image. The word on the street, passed eagerly from one to another, was that he'll be "gay for pay," but that in all of his films, he only *received* anal sex once, because he thinks *real* men aren't sexually passive, or "bottoms" in the vernacular. This is more nonsense.

I chose not to go to this porn star's show. I'm not particularly impressed with big penises. Ray and I are both sufficiently endowed that, for the sake of comfort, anal sex has never been popular in our household. But I wouldn't go out of my way and pay to see a guy with big genitalia. I fear that it would feel too much like a side show at a carnival, and that I would end up liking myself less for going.

For me, today, the most exciting sexual scenario is having my body lovingly and sensuously explored by another, and being allowed to do the same with a body that attracts or interests me. I like to take my time with sex, to smell, look, touch, and taste at will. I like putting my head on a man's chest and listening to his heart beat. I like having permission and giving permission for pure pleasure-seeking.

Ray likes the gentle touch too. His nipples are sensitive, as are his testicles. He wants them touched softly and caringly, not roughly. He doesn't much like performing fellatio. He'd rather receive it. I, on the other hand, enjoy receiving it, but would much rather give it. Doing so is a major "turn-on" for me.

Is this too much information (TMI)? Is it too explicit or too personal? Gosh, I hope not, particularly in a book by a sexuality educator. As every sex therapist, counselor, and educator knows, the biggest obstacles to sexual health and maturity for everyone across the globe are *secrecy, ignorance,* and *trauma.* If we can't talk about sex openly, it becomes "dirty." If it's "dirty," we remain *ignorant.* If we're ignorant, we're prime targets for *trauma* (such as getting arrested for soliciting sex in a men's room at the airport). That's why I think that it's important to discuss it. If I'm honest here about my experiences, maybe I can spare one or two other people sexual trauma in their lives. Ignorance is *not* bliss.

When Ray and I first had sex, it began with a lot of kissing and gently stroking each other's penis. He would then get on top of me and start moving his body up and down on mine, creating exciting friction on our aroused genitals, until he reached orgasm. When he was relaxed and at peace, we would change positions and engage in the same "frottage," or body-rubbing, until I reached orgasm. We'd also step into the shower with one another, make love in the woods, and make out in the car. In our twenties, we each got immediately aroused when we touched the other, even if it was only holding hands while one was driving.

In the beginning, though our sex was frequent and very pleasurable, we didn't tell each other what felt good, and we both silently endured small discomforts and disappointments. We didn't know that it was not only *okay* to talk about what did or didn't give us pleasure, but *necessary* for an ongoing, sexually-satisfying relationship. We also didn't know that it was okay to say that having sex at certain times, such as when one or both of us was intoxicated was rarely, if ever, satisfying.

Eventually, our sex became a bit routine and less frequent, so we tried to enhance it with marijuana, and then with "poppers," the second of which increases the heart rate and focuses the mind on touch. We lit incense and candles, put on the song "Bolero" from the film *10*, and swooned in our independent fantasies. The "grass" worked better than the poppers. Sniffing the amyl nitrate eventually required ever-increasing use to maintain the "high," which interrupted the excitement more than it enhanced it. So we quit using the poppers and looked for other means to keep the sex as exciting as it originally was.

After a few years, I found myself fantasizing about making love to other people while I was making love to Ray. He did the same, but with less frequency. Initially, my behavior scared me because I felt that fantasizing about others might mean that we were headed for a break up of the relationship. But, actually, the opposite was true. Such fantasizing, at least for me, diminished the compulsive interest I might have had in a person other than Ray, and neither the fantasized person nor Ray were aware of what was going on in my mind. When I let go of the guilt, the fantasies became less frequent.

At one point in our relationship, we began experimenting by inviting other people to join us in the bedroom. (One stayed for two years.) We found that each time we did so, it enhanced our intimacy as well as the quality of the sex we later had together. When a third person was present, Ray and I would maintain eye contact with each other and hold hands. Later, we would always reach the conclusion that an occasional threesome experience can be fun but anything more frequent is too complicated and disruptive to our relationship.

Sex with Ray was always enjoyable while he was able to get an erection. If I could arouse him, even if it took more patience and time, our love-making was mutually satisfying. When medications, depleted testosterone, and a minimized interest in sex impacted his ability to perform, we eventually quit making the attempt. It was too frustrating or embarrassing for us both.

But we always talked about it. Since we first came together, we have both committed ourselves to talking through our feelings about everything, if not initially about sex. We learned with practice that sometimes we have had to wait until one or the other of us felt safe enough to talk. Sometimes we've needed the help of a therapist to do so. Sometimes the talking happened at the wrong moment, such as when one was on his way out the door on a road trip, or on the telephone at work, just before guests arrived for the weekend, or right before lights were turned off for bed. So we learned that success depended upon timing. And we also had to learn that *how* you say something, even "I'm sorry," dramatically impacts the ability of the other person to listen and respond rationally. But there was no subject off-limits, and this practice of honest, open communication not only enhanced our sex life, but continues to make the relationship feel vital and worth the work we have to put into it.

Talking about what made us feel good sexually was harder to learn and to do in a non-threatening way than talking about anything else, including our feelings about each other's family. But we worked really hard at it, because we knew it was important. Talking about sex, but not during the love-making, is what enabled us to learn from the other what felt good and what didn't, what we liked to do and what we liked to have done to us, what our experiences of the past had been and what our sexual fantasies included, how it felt to see another person being pleasured by the other and how jealousy was impacting us outside of the bedroom, what it felt like not to get an erection and what it felt like to have your partner be limp. Today we're talking about how to make sure we maintain touch and intimacy in the relationship, and how to ensure that each of our sexual needs are met. The other night, for instance, as we watched a television program about a married man who had a mistress, Ray said, "You know, it's completely okay with me if you'd like to have someone on the side."

As I have previously stated, I don't feel the same about him having an affair. Jealousy makes me behave like the love child of the Glenn Close character from *Fatal Attraction* and the Jack Nicholson character from *The Shining*. I'm not happy with the emotion, but I'm learning to make friends with it.

Recent studies have shown that men and women, regardless of their orientation, are sexually active into their seventies and eighties. I intend to be, and Ray and I hold out hope that with time and an adjustment of medications he too will be. Right now it means less to him than it does to me. Whatever we do, though, we're going to do it together, giving each other the encouragement to explore what feels good and makes each of us happy.

Just as we don't count on others to tell us what sex act makes us *real* men or *truly* gay, we don't want someone else telling us what feels good or will make us happy. Nor should anyone else, gay, lesbian, bisexual, or straight, who wants to truly enjoy a lifetime of sexual health.

16

My snowy white hair hung nearly as low as my beard, which fell to the middle of my chest. Wireless glasses perched at the end of my nose. I ambled slowly, supported by a tall walking stick. For the ten hours that I was Merlin, I really loved being old.

The theme for Carnival in Provincetown was "Fairy Tales." One hundred and twenty thousand spectators lined Commercial Street on that beautiful, slightly windy Thursday of the third week in August, to cheer as costumed storybook characters and floats made their way from the East to the West End of town. Ahead of me and behind me there were several young men clad only in gold lame' bikinis, strutting their Adonis bodies for all to behold. Their connection to a "Fairy Tale" escaped me, but our different costumes probably had a lot to do with our age, our bodies, and our marital status. If I was their age, had their bodies, and was single, I'd want to "strut my stuff " in a gold lame' bikini too.

I didn't want to take off my sorcerer's black cap, cloak, and cape, nor the bag which had carried 150 "magical" rings I had handed out to wide-eyed children, who promised "to use them wisely." Though my costume made me of less interest to the gay male spectators who were looking for a "turn on," it wasn't their attention that I sought. I wanted to tickle the fancy of those whose smiles, like mine, always broaden with the image of age-old knowledge in the persona of characters like Yoda, Gandalf, and Dumbledore.

The next day at dinner, a visiting 39-year-old, partnered friend was lamenting his impending birthday. "I don't *want* to be 40," he whined. "I want to be a *Twinkie.*"

The assembled group gently called his attention to the fact that he hadn't been a Twinkie in over 15 years. "Twinkies," in the gay community, are generally considered to be gay males between the ages of 18 and 24, like those in the parade, whose focus is having a good time and whose good looks and trim, slightly muscular bodies are their tickets to the "Fun House." Their day jobs are less important to them than their nights out. Their bank rolls are of much less concern to them than their belly rolls. They know that if they remain cute and thin enough, someone older, wiser, and wealthier will buy them their drinks, their drugs, and just maybe a shiny red convertible.

Not all young adult gay men are Twinkies, but too many people who are well past the appropriate age still want to either be one or have one. These older men yearn to be young because they equate sexual gratification with a youthful body, and they equate having a good time with having youthful looks. That's why so many older guys regrettably buy from catalogues, such as *International Male*, clothes that are modeled by handsome, buffed men in their twenties. They hope that wearing the same fishnet t-shirt will allow them to blend into, and be accepted by, the younger crowd. They generally have no idea of how sad they appear to others, young and old alike.

The visiting friend at dinner continued with his lament, "Gay life *ends* at 40." He was speaking to a group of gay men whose ages ranged from 46 to 60. Our groans were audible in Boston, a two-hour drive away.

Many gay men, particularly those who are single, seem to have great fear about aging. They snidely refer to the bars where older gay men congregate as "the wrinkle room." They live in dread that one day they too will become their image of old age -- a booze-slurring, jewelry-laden letch with sagging breasts and butt who spends his time sexually harassing young men and watching re-runs of *The Golden Girls*. I've met some older gay men like that, but most of the older gay men and women I know, especially those who are coupled, have full, happy, and very satisfying lives, and *none* of them would exchange it for being in their twenties again.

Ray and I actually love being the ages we are, and our gay life now is more fun and more fulfilling than it *ever* was before. We feel we have grown into our bodies and that we are better looking today than we have ever been. We like each other's graying hair and we're drawn to each other's maturity. We each believe that humans are called to age gracefully, like all other forms of life, and embrace the process as nature's intention.

In the "autumn" of our journeys, Ray and I feel we now have the good sense and the good cents to enjoy the entire menu of life. We no longer worry about pimples, we don't fret about being liked, we aren't competing with other people's bodies, and we don't live in dread of being asked how old we are.

Being young, it seems to me, is a matter of attitude, not age. "Old" is twenty years more than you are now. One's youthful mind lasts a lot longer than one's muscled chest and flat stomach.

I'm actually *not* sexually attracted to Twinkies, or emotionally drawn to people who *want* to be Twinkies. The idea of having sex with someone who could be my son doesn't appeal to me at all. I understand why it does to others, given the smoothness of the skin and the firmness of the bodies, but people that much younger than me have never "turned me on." And the thought of trying to create a stable romantic relationship with someone in their twenties or thirties when I'm in my sixties makes me tired.

I lament how much time many gay men spend fearing growing old. It's a useless exercise and the stress creates wrinkles.

Bette Davis said "Getting old is not for sissies." But she was talking about the faint of heart, not men who love men, and she was referring to the physical challenges, not the emotional or spiritual ones.

The hardest part about getting old for Ray and for me is that our bodies are a bit less cooperative than they once were. For instance, it's harder to lose weight. You more frequently fall asleep while reading. And the hairs in your ears grow more vigorously than you ever imagined possible. So, we compensate. We eat less and exercise more. We take more naps. And we spend more time with tweezers in front of the magnifying mirror.

Ray has always been a very active man. He loved doing tasks that required climbing on ladders and roof tops, and under cars and houses. He seemingly could lift any weight, twist his body in any direction, and manage any physical challenge he faced to maintain our homes. Now he can't do all of that as easily or as well. His hands have slight tremors, he has arthritis and neuropathy in his limbs, and he is often debilitated by muscle spasms in his back and neck.

He and I used to run five miles each day, but we both tore the meniscus in our right knees and so we now walk five miles each morning. Ray used to take delight in trimming the hedges around our homes but he now asks, and is grateful, for help from friends who have fewer ailments. You learn to adjust when you get older. Like an older dog, you chase fewer cats.

Ray's and my sex together, as I have previously said, was very satisfying until a couple of years ago when Ray's erections became less dependable. Coping with his erectile dysfunction was a significant emotional challenge for Ray and for me. He felt his manhood was compromised by his inability to please me sexually and be pleased himself. That took some time for us to make peace with, but we've learned other ways to communicate our passion for one another, just as a person who loses a sense, such as seeing, compensates by strengthening another, such as hearing.

Far more challenging to me than the loss of our mutual orgasms was the diagnosis of prostate cancer that I got a couple of years ago. I hadn't been in the hospital with anything seriously wrong with me since I was a child with pneumonia, an experience I don't even remember. The word "cancer" can be really frightening. It momentarily knocked the wind out of me when I heard the doctor say "Brian, the test came back positive." I started thinking about how much time I had left and what I would do with it. But after Ray and I did some research on the Internet, and I talked to the best doctors I could find, I realized that I probably wouldn't die from prostate cancer, that I wouldn't become incontinent or impotent, and that with the right procedure, I would be as good as new in no time. They planted a couple dozen radioactive titanium seeds in my prostate at Beth Israel Hospital in Boston, and since then I've had perfect check-ups and no difficulties, unless you count setting off the Geiger counter at U.S. Customs, causing me to be pulled out of line and questioned by three people.

The inconveniences of aging have been really minor for us. Our "ripened" bodies, for instance, didn't stop Ray and me from kayaking and sleeping in tents for a week in the Galapagos last year, and then flying to meet Tom and David in Peru where we spent a week climbing and sleeping on the Inca Trail as we made our way up and down 13,000 foot mountains to Machu Pichu. Climbing in and out of the tents, though, prompted us to donate all of our camping gear at the end of the trek to the porters, as we didn't think we would use them again. Nevertheless, we left feeling that old age had failed to make "sissies" out of any of us.

One aspect of aging that takes more thought and adjustment than we had imagined is the related issue of retirement. Ray retired when he was 45, but only after preparing himself with several sessions of therapy, and even then, it took him and me at least two years to settle into it.

The hardest part about retiring, I believe, is defining who you now are to yourself and to others. At least on the East Coast of the United States, social interactions often begin with the question "What do you do for work?" The questioner is looking for common ground on which to connect, but often the retiree questioned experiences the query as a judgment of value. "I *do* nothing," feels as if you're saying "I *am* nothing." Ray had a really tough time with that one. His initial response of "I'm retired and am now on a spiritual journey," scared people, which was unsettling for him. Now he knows that their discomfort with his status is *their* issue, not his.

For some reason, I have an easier time saying the words "I'm an alcoholic," than saying "I'm retiring." So I don't say it. I keep flirting with the idea of no longer accepting speaking engagements and corporate training sessions, but I can't imagine myself not working. Perhaps it's my ego. I'd like to think it's my desire to make a difference in other people's lives.

Beyond the issue of self-esteem, the other problem created by retirement is the change that is required in an individual's, and in a couple's, daily life. I've worked out of the house for much of the past thirty-plus years. For most of that time, Ray left for the office by 6 a.m. and returned by 7 p.m. Then suddenly, he was home for lunch, ready to play, and wanting to take over some of the household responsibilities that had given my life meaning. "What do you *mean* I don't fold the napkins and towels the *right* way?" We've worked through all of that, and have found a wonderful new rhythm for our relationship that works for us both. I now love having him home for lunch, to play, and to fold the laundry.

The true joy of Ray's and my gay life as older men is the abundant amount of quality time we have to ourselves and with each other. We are free to expend as many hours and as much energy as we choose pondering the meaning of life, doing a crossword puzzle, creating meals, designing and tending the gardens, reading books, traveling, swimming and sunning, watching movies, talking through feelings, fishing, planning parties, touring art museums, antiquing, sleeping, watching birds, writing, and being with friends. Young gay people can do all of that too, but much of it doesn't yet interest them, and if it does, they don't have the time to do any of it with leisure.

Ray's and my mornings begin at 5:30 and 6, respectively. Ray heads downstairs for coffee and meditation. I check e-mail, cnn. com, and sports scores. I make the bed, brush my teeth and shave, do sit-ups and push-ups, and then go downstairs for an energy drink, a reading from the Tao, and recitation of the prayer of St. Francis of Assisi. We then walk for five miles, drink a "smoothie," read the *New York Times* and *Boston Globe* or Ft. Lauderdale *Sun-Sentinel*, do a crossword puzzle, go for a swim, and head to our respective home offices for investment work on his part, and writing on mine. He does housework and I head to the garden where I mow the lawn, weed, and cut flowers for the table.

We regroup at lunch for fresh fruit and low-fat cottage cheese, work on another crossword puzzle, return to tasks such as preparation of dinner or organizing photos, then read in bed, and take a nap. In the evening, we either set up tables in front of the television and watch programs we've taped, or we join Tom and David, or other friends, for dinner and games.

Each Sunday night, for instance, we get together with Tom and David, and Ann and Harriet for dinner (and a dark chocolate dessert) at each other's homes and play Hearts. On Wednesday, we get together with Tom and David, and Gregg and Scott for dinner (and a dark chocolate dessert) and play Mexican Train. On both nights, though none of us drink, other than David and Harriet who will each have one small glass of wine, we laugh so hard that we cry and close the doors and windows so as not to disturb the neighbors.

We go crazy with gifts at each other's birthdays and Christmas, and gather for a festive meal for all holidays. We have more friends too – Kath and Kim, Jean and Chip, Sharon and Patsy, and Michael, among others, with whom we play bocce on the lawn, have bonfire meals at the beach, go to movies, take the boat out for picnics and lobstering, and do water ballet in the pool.

When young people, gay and straight, spend time with our small family, they generally say, "We want what *you've* got. You guys

127

have so much *fun* together. That's what I want my life to be like."
But when we were their age, we weren't playing Mexican Train.
Instead, we were taking a quick nap at 8 p.m. so that we could get
up and be at the bar by 10 p.m. We didn't know how to make fools
of ourselves without the help of drugs and alcohol, so instead we
generally said and did things we later regretted, and we woke up
feeling sick. We didn't laugh with abandon. Instead we were too
worried about how we looked. Sometimes, we practiced laughing in
front of the mirror.

Our bodies were a bit thinner and our hair was a bit thicker when
we were in our twenties, we had less gas and we talked less about
what medications we were taking, we imagined ourselves as Luke
Skywalker rather than Yoda and young Harry Potter rather than
Dumbledore, but we weren't much at peace with ourselves or the
world in which we lived. All of our gay and lesbian friends today
who are older, as I said, would love to have bodies that belonged
in gold lame' bikinis that got leering looks and tickets to the "Fun
House." But, they wouldn't trade the serenity they have found in
their lives, serenity that is only possible through many years of
lived experiences, for any of it. That's why they, and the very young
children, smiled so happily at Merlin as he walked slowly by and
entrusted others with special, enchanted rings. They knew *that's*
where they would find the magic.

17

As was (and is) undoubtedly true for most youngsters across the globe, being told that there was no such thing as Santa Claus was a *very* unwelcome end to the best fantasy of my childhood. For me, it was like the slap across the buttocks that Ray and I each got upon our exit from the quiet warmth of our mothers' wombs. I *really* didn't want to let go of something that had made me feel so safe and so very special.

Life is full of such big disappointments, I know. They can weaken us or they can strengthen us. For me, they do *both*, first through the personal disappointment and then by the strengthening of character and resolve. That's especially true for our relationships with others. The disappointments we experience initially make us sad and angry, and then they make us more independent and self-actualized. If we aren't slapped, we might not start breathing on our own. And the slaps of awakening don't stop at birth or at the truth about Santa Claus.

For instance, Ray and I both grew up as Irish (his mom was a Gorman), Catholic, Democrat, American members of Midwestern families. Each one of those cherished categories created for us a sense of true belonging, boundless pride, and great comfort. And each and every one of them caused us enormous sadness and debilitating anger because of our profound disappointment with them.

Let's start with being Irish. I *loved* being Irish and saying that I was Irish when I was a teenager. The world, I was told, was divided between those who were Irish and those who *wished* they were Irish. We Irish had shamrocks and leprechauns, Fr. O'Malley in *Going My Way,* and the Kennedys in the White House, brogues and shillelaghs, "Oh Danny Boy" and McNamara's Band. We were the *best*, as far as I was concerned.

But, my grandfather McNaught used to whisper as we sang "When Irish Eyes Are Smiling," that "you won't be so proud when you run into the *South Boston* Irish." Regrettably, he was right. After I witnessed their violent response to busing, their stubborn barring of gay people from the St. Patrick's Day Parade, and the lack of equanimity that characterized the former mayor and Vatican ambassador, Ray Flynn, in his anti-gay marriage crusade, I lost my romanticism about, and pride in, the Irish. The truth is, I'm actually only part Irish anyway. The McNaught side was probably originally Scottish, Mom's dad was English, and Dad's mom was French. Reluctantly at first, and then with genuine relief, I came to enjoy identifying myself as a cultural mutt without allegiances to or let-downs by any one group.

The once-beloved influence of the revered Roman Catholic Church on our lives, and its subsequent demise, was, of course, the biggest source of emotional let down for me and Ray. It caused soul-wrenching sadness and heart-breaking disappointment for us.

I loved being Catholic and *saying* that I was Catholic. It was fun and prestigious, at least in my mind. "Come home to Rome," we Catholics would say and pray. Every other religion to us was an "also-ran." I used to tease my Episcopal priest partner, Dan, by saying, "The founder of my religion died on a cross. How did the founder of your religion die?"

Everyone in the world, I imagined, loved John Kennedy, a Catholic. Everyone in the world, we thought, loved Pope John XXIII, a Catholic. And, did you see Loretta Young as a nun in *Come to the Stable,* and Rosalind Russell in *The Trouble with Angels,* and Audrey Hepburn in *The Nun's Story?* The hills and our hearts were alive with *The Sound of Music.*

The Second Vatican Council affirmed every value Ray and I held dear, particularly its insistence on the presence of the Holy Spirit's wisdom in each person's life. The revelation of God's will could and did come from any of us. It was a time of great vibrancy in the Church. But then, almost overnight, it felt as if the Ecumenical Council had never happened. Pope John XXIII was replaced by Pope Paul VI who issued an encyclical on birth control that made *no* sense to anyone other than conservative theologians. That document was responsible for the departure of thousands of priests and nuns from their ministry. Pope John Paul II followed in his socially conservative footsteps, guided throughout his reign by arch conservative Cardinal Joseph Ratzinger, who became Pope Benedict XVI. Both of these men enforced strict adherence to papal authority. They, and the many bishops who supported them, further depleted the Church of nearly all of its free-thinking Catholics. They consciously made Ray and me, and millions of others, feel completely unwelcome in the Church of our birth. But they also simultaneously *freed* us from the cultural bondage to, and baggage of, a religion that had ceased to have meaning in our everyday lives as gay men. Initially, we wandered aimlessly as frightened orphans through a labyrinth of religious beliefs, but eventually we found a home and a security in a spirituality that didn't require a membership. Thus, we would never again feel excluded or rejected by a religious community.

Though my father was a Nixon Republican, I've always been a Democrat. The same is true for Ray. We've only voted for one Republican in our lives, when the GOP candidate for Governor of Massachusetts was far more supportive of us than the intolerant Democrat with the gay son. We've always donated financially to the party even when we couldn't afford it, we posted signs in front of our homes even when they were repeatedly defaced by neighbors, we cried during moving, inclusive keynote addresses at the Democratic National Conventions, and we stayed up most of the night with upset stomachs watching with enormous anxiety the result of local, state, and national elections. Not so much anymore. While we still watch election returns because we and the country, in our opinion, are better off with Democrats in control of the White House and Congress, we've lost our passion for, and trust in the party as a whole.

We're not disappointed with Republicans because we don't *expect* anything from them. But as was true with the Irish and with the Catholic Church, we have had very high expectations of Democratic candidates for executive office. And with the exception of a handful of people who regrettably don't have much of a chance to be elected President, Democratic politicians are generally weak-kneed on gay issues, reading polls before they take a public stand on topics such as gay marriage. For many of them, their private rationale is "I believe in gay marriage but I'll never get elected if I openly support it. Let me support civil unions and then, when I'm in office, I'll say what I *really* think." Then it's, "Let me first secure a second term." And then it's "I've got my legacy to think about."

Though nearly all of our political heroes are Democrats, we're very disappointed in the party as a whole. Yet, we're no longer emotionally crushed by the party's lack of leadership on behalf of gay, lesbian, bisexual, and transgender people. We've grown up a bit, and have become a little more politically sophisticated.

Regarding the country as a whole, Ray and I are both very grateful to have been born in the United States of America. We hang flags and bunting on all major national holidays and we sing the national anthem with great enthusiasm. On the Fourth of July, we vigorously clap as the veterans, Coast Guard, firefighters, police officers and emergency medical service personnel march by in Provincetown's wonderful small town parade, and on Veteran's Day, we give thanks before our meals for the sacrifices made by others to ensure our civil liberties. We love the Stars and Stripes, democracy, free enterprise, the exquisite beauty of this land, the history of our civil rights struggles, the goodness and generosity of many of our people, and all of the freedoms we are guaranteed by our Constitution and by local, state, and federal laws, including my right to make love to Ray, an act that would result in us being hanged, beheaded, or imprisoned in other parts of the world.

Ray and I have had the great luxury of traveling to 49 of the 50 states (Oregon, we'll make it) and to almost every continent. We know London as well as we know New York. We've run out of places that we want to see or where we feel safe as gay men or as Americans. Our experience in traveling the globe underscores how extraordinarily fortunate we are to be Americans. But, as hard as it would be to do, we are at an age and at a point in our lives, where we would consider leaving the U.S. if the country and our government continue their unwelcoming behavior and attitudes toward gay people. We've grown weary of listening to others debate with gratuitous hostility whether we are fit to be parents, be Boy Scouts, be soldiers, or be married.

We cringe with embarrassment at the time of this writing, that gay people in Uruguay have more civil rights than we gay people do in the United States. We have been continually let down by U.S. presidents who ignored the epidemic of AIDS until 40,000 gay Americans had been diagnosed with HIV, who actively opposed the decriminalization of same-sex behavior, and who used gay marriage as an emotional wedge to politically divide our families and friends. We expected *far* more of the leadership of this nation. But, our sadness and our anger at our government actually free us not to need a nationality or a flag to affirm our identity. Ray's and my primary responsibilities in this life are to ourselves and then to each other and to others. If we ultimately decide that we are physically and emotionally safer living in another land, we will very reluctantly leave the country. We've threatened to do so during the Reagan and Bush presidencies, but we now feel more emotionally capable of making the break. We don't want to go but we could.

When Ray was growing up in Kansas and I was growing up in Michigan we each loved our home states very much. Since we merged our lives, we have visited each other's birthplaces on several occasions, often because of anniversaries, weddings, and funerals. I understand why Ray would have enjoyed his childhood in Wichita and he appreciates why I have happy memories of Flint, Grand Blanc, and Birmingham. But neither of us feels pride today in our home states, and neither of us would willingly move back to them.

The Midwest, like the Irish, the Catholic Church, the Democratic Party, and America had an endearing reputation when we were youngsters that made us proud to be from Kansas and Michigan. Midwesterners were thought to be the friendliest people in the country, and the hardest working. You knew in college or at work that when you told people where you were from they would relax and smile because you weren't from the crazy East or West coast. As Midwesterners, you were thought to be stable, reliable, and good-hearted - the salt of the earth.

While all of that is still undoubtedly true, it's also true that the people in my home state and the people in Ray's home state have voted in large majorities to deny our marriage any legal recognition. For us today, it's hard to say we're from a state, much less go back to live in one, which is willing to bar its own people from receiving basic civil rights. So, we no longer feel any attachment to Kansas, to Michigan, or to any state, for that matter.

And then there's family. Our families were the source of our identity and of our security when we were young. Being a "Struble boy" and "one of the McNaughts" meant we belonged to a well-respected and much-liked clan, unique in its size and personality. We each privately worried what might happen to our sense of security if the other Strubles and the other McNaughts learned of our attraction to men. Would we still be Strubles and McNaughts?

When we came out, Ray was told "Leave this house. You are on your own," and I was told initially "You'll outgrow it," and then "Do you have any idea how much pain you're putting us through? If you go on that television show, you won't be allowed back into this house."

Both sets of parents came around to welcoming us each home. Irish humor, Catholic forgiveness, political fair-mindedness, American perseverance, and Midwestern good sense worked together to help us all get through the crisis. But our families were never the same, our roles in our families changed, and our

135

experience of "family" was forever altered. That is perhaps true for members of many families as each person ages and begins to live his or her own life. Family traditions are abandoned or fade away. Expectations diminish. But when you're gay, at least from our perspective, and you find yourself being disenfranchised from so many other sources of security, such as the country or the Church, the sense of alienation from *family* becomes acute. And if you feel that your sexuality is being *accommodated* and not *affirmed*, that your logical family is being *tolerated* but not *celebrated*, then you drift away not only from your biological family but also its hold on your identity. I'm a McNaught, but I don't feel now that I owe my family any more allegiance than I do to the Catholic Church or to the State of Michigan.

The independence that Ray and I feel from all of the primary sources of our childhood identity empowers us now to become the people we are called to be. Years ago, a national Catholic magazine asked me to address the issue, "Are gay people part of God's plan?" I wrote that when I die, I imagine that God will ask me "Brian, did you sing the song I taught you?" My song has been influenced by my being an Irish, Catholic, Democratic, American, Midwestern McNaught but I'm far more than any of that.

My song has also been profoundly impacted by the fact that I'm gay. Can we continue to talk about disappointment?

When Ray and I first came out, like most every gay person I know, we had *enormous*, unrealistic expectations of the gay community, now known by some as the gay, lesbian, bisexual, transgender, queer, and questioning community. If we were going to be rejected by the Irish, the Catholics, the Democrats, America, the Midwest and our biological families, at least, we thought, we would feel safe and secure in our new home, the "community" of other gay men and women. These people would know our pain. They would know what it's like to be frightened, isolated, lonely, harassed, and abused. Their leaders would be thoughtful and generous with their time and their praise of us. The bar owners and managers would be welcoming and comforting. The writers, comedians, singers, and other standard bearers would help elevate us to a higher level of living where we would swell with pride about who we were and about the great contribution that we were making to the world as homosexuals.

There were many truly wonderful people who did just that, but they were outnumbered by those who, in their own pain, added to our fear, loneliness, harassment, and abuse. The great sadness and anger we felt at the "gay community" when our high expectations were not met further isolated us from others. On the one hand, that was a horribly disappointing and depressing experience. On the other hand, though, it forced us to look to ourselves and to each other for meaning, for love, for security, for comfort, and for guidance. Our relationship of love was strengthened by the adversity and disappointment we encountered inside and outside of the gay community. For that, we're both eternally grateful.

The *Tao* reading this morning said, "When there is no desire, all things are at peace."

I know that I created the suffering in my life by my clinging and my desire. I was upset because I wanted to stay in the womb. I was sad because I wanted to continue to believe in Santa Claus. As a multiply-blessed child, I was free to be a romantic and so I had storybook images of my Church, my country, and my family. I *really* believed that if I was as good as I could be, none of them would let me down. My intense desire for acceptance and security eliminated any chance of me finding peace. My unrealistic expectations of the major influences in my life made me suffer terribly.

As I reflect on my disappointments, I become aware of how much sadness and anger I regrettably must have created in the lives of others who didn't want me to be gay or outspoken. My career as a gay educator was a disappointment to my parents. Ray leaving the seminary was a disappointment to his.

This book alone is bound to cause enormous let down for many people -- my family members who expected that I would never tell embarrassing secrets, gay Catholics who thought I would never leave the Church, monogamous gay and lesbian couples who assumed that Ray and I were genitally exclusive, and corporate diversity officers who thought that they had a messenger without any controversy in his life.

I hate being a disappointment to others. In light of my daily petition in the Prayer of St. Francis to be a source of peace, love, pardon, faith, hope, light, and joy, it is particularly unsettling to think that I might be the source of another's hatred, injury, doubt, despair, darkness, or sadness. I apologize sincerely for any sadness or anger that others experience because I wasn't who or what they wanted me to be. But, if I have learned anything in my sixty-plus years, it is that our freedom to become whole comes at the price of letting go of our expectations, even one as seemingly noble as making everyone happy. It's an unwanted slap on the buttocks but it forces us to breathe. As St. Francis said, "It is in dying that we're born to eternal life."

The life that Ray and I have found together on our journeys as a gay male couple has required that we experience the death of our expectations and subsequently, of other parts of our identities. At least, that's the song that I feel our God has taught us to sing.

18

In my youth, one of my favorite "brain teasers" in the magazines I read, was the one that challenged me to find a variety of objects hidden in a picture. "Can you find and circle the dog, the cat, the horn, the piece of pie, the pipe, the monkey, and the alarm clock?"

The "soul teaser" for me now is to find and circle, in the full and very accurate picture of this day (as I have experienced it), just one thing. "Can you find God?"

The morning began for me with a reading from the *Tao te Ching*, the single book I would take with me to a desert island, if I was allowed the choice of only one.

"The Tao doesn't take sides; it gives birth to both good and evil.

The Master doesn't take sides; she welcomes both saints and sinners.

The Tao is like a bellows: it is empty yet infinitely capable.

The more you use it, the more it produces;

The more you talk of it, the less you understand.

Hold on to the Center."

Ray began his morning by sitting in meditation on a cushion, facing the garden and the sea beyond, his eyes cast downward, his hands on his folded legs, his thoughts quieted by the focus on his breath.

As I sipped the hot drink Ray had prepared for me, I read and re-read the Prayer of St. Francis of Assisi, as I do each morning. It's printed on the back of my mother's funeral card. I re-read it because my mind drifted off and I wanted to be sure that I focused on my daily intention.

"Lord make me an instrument of Your peace; where there is hatred, let me sow love; where there is injury, pardon; where there is doubt, faith; where there is despair, hope; where there is darkness, light; and where there is sadness, joy.

"O Divine Master, grant that I may not so much seek to be consoled, as to console; to be understood as to understand; to be loved, as to love; for it is in giving that we receive, it is in pardoning that we are pardoned, and it is in dying that we are born to eternal life."

Ray and I then walked together, mostly in silence, through five miles of national seashore. The rolling hills of sand were covered in a blanket of gold, brown, and red grasses, beach plumbs, rose hips, and poison ivy, all letting go of their summer lives in the brilliant morning light. We waved and smiled at each runner, bicyclist, fellow walker, and driver. "Good morning!"

The majestic beauty of the terrain prompts the mute singing of a song Ray and I learned at a Mass for gay Catholics, "*Holy,* Lord is your name in the heavens above. Blessed be the Lord's name, sing His glory forever: Holy, holy the Lord, for He dwells in our land."

After our traditional breakfast of a smoothie with orange juice, fruit, and non-fat yogurt, followed by the *New York Times* crossword puzzle, when we tease each other about making a mess with our wrong answers, I answered e-mail. One was from a 49-year-old priest who said he was gay, had never had sex, but was finding it almost impossible to endure the hypocrisy of the closet in a Church that didn't want his services.

I then walked to my bi-weekly massage which was made more "other-worldly" by the extraordinarily moving Gregorian chant sung by Benedictine monks. The combination of deep, healing touch, the smell of rosemary, and the mesmerizing musical praise for the divine carried me away into a pampered zone of peace. I climaxed the experience with an orgasm and a smile of gratitude.

I cut up fresh fruit for the lunch we shared, sitting side by side at the table that overlooks the purple lace-cap hydrangeas, the bird feeders loaded with hungry yellow finches, and the statue of Buddha, arms raised in a grand belly laugh. I put low-fat vanilla yogurt on the Bartlett pair, grapes, and roasted peanuts, the two percent milkfat cottage cheese next to the sliced peach, and carefully arranged the chunks of watermelon nearby. The fruit this summer has been wonderful. We held hands as we do before every meal, and I said, "Spirit of life, we're very grateful for this meal, for the love we share, for the time we have together, and for all of our blessings.

We send out our hearts to those we know are less fortunate than we. Amen"

As Ray headed up to his computer to organize photos of our trip to Venice, I swam the fifty yards out to our boat, a 19-foot Grady White with a 1987 hull and a new 115-horse power Evinrude motor. I started it up, attached the depth finder, unhooked the mooring, and slowly guided it through the other moored boats, lobster traps, and kayakers, and headed to the harbor, where all of the old fishing trawlers creaked as they rocked in their berths, and where the massive, recreated pirate ship lowered it sails. Whale watching boats glided by me as the naturalist on board told the eager passengers about the humpback whales, mystical in my mind, that they would see today feeding with their calves at Stillwagen Bank.

After I left the "no wake" zone, I opened up the throttle to full speed and let the warm wind blow in my face as I sped through small waves to the Long Point lighthouse at the very tip of the Cape. From there, I set out to investigate a giant green buoy well off shore that I had never noticed before. In the center of its metal frame sat a beautiful old bell and three large clappers. I guessed that in major storms the bell would clang loudly from the movement of the waves and warn approaching ships of the sandbars nearby. There were few waves today, so I circled the buoy several times in my boat and created enough turbulence that it responded with a deep, church bell sound. I burst out laughing with genuine glee.

Upon my return home, I found in the mail a book that had been sent by Steven Tierney, a gay male friend who also has a hunger for meaningful spiritual practice and wanted to share his discovery of *Happiness – A Guide to Developing Life's Most Important Skill.* I left it on the counter and headed up to the third floor where I turned down the bed for our afternoon nap. Before nodding off to sleep, I read a few more pages of Deepak Chopra's book *Buddha –A Story of Enlightenment.* I had left off where Gautama, previously known as Siddhartha, had carried his hunger-ravaged body to the base of a tree where he planned to meditate. Upon opening his eyes, he encountered Mara, the chief manifestation of evil, who tried every trick he could conceive to lure the future Buddha from his path.

After closing the book, I looked over at Ray, who had already dozed off beside me, and I marveled at his beauty and his goodness, which I often do when I watch him sleep.

Upon awakening 45 minutes later, I quietly got dressed, went to my computer, and began chronicling the day.

Now, can you find and circle God in this picture of my perfect day?

Which God? Who's God? I see the Tao. I see Buddha. I see God the Father. I see Jesus. I see Gaia, our Mother Earth.

When one asks me, "Can you find God?" do they mean the manifestations of the divine? I see love. I see thoughtfulness and generosity. I see physical pleasure. I see holiness. I see beauty. I see pure joy. I see a life enjoyed and appreciated.

And the day wasn't really all that seemingly perfect. Some people didn't smile or wave back at us on our walk. We had to step over dog poop that some irresponsible owner had left behind. My e-mail folder was filled with junk. The massage therapist had to avoid the very tender finger on my left hand that I had smashed in the refrigerator door the day before. The water I swam through was loaded with seaweed for the first five feet off shore. A couple people in speed boats came directly at me and I had to maneuver to avoid them. The mail also had some bills. And a dog barked through my nap. But I didn't really focus on any of that. Wisdom is knowing what to overlook.

If you had presented me a picture in my childhood, in my adolescence, and in my young adulthood and asked me to find God, I would have looked carefully for three figures - a kindly old man with long white hair and a beard, a bearded younger man who was either hanging on a cross or showing his sacred heart, and a dove with its wings spread: Father, Son, and Holy Spirit. Nothing else would be recognized as divine or circled.

In college, Ray and I, independent of each other, read the same books on Eastern religion and entertained the same doubts about Christianity providing the only path to God, the historic accuracy of the Old Testament, the truth of the infancy narrative, the reliability of the recording of Jesus' words, and the authority of the pope. So if you asked us then to find God in a picture of multiple images, we would have defiantly circled more than just the Christian symbols.

The spiritual holocaust we experienced as gay men at the hands of religious fundamentalists - Christian, Jew, and Muslim - knocked the Jesus out of us, as well as any trust in religious authority. We both left the Catholic Church because of its caste system (we were "untouchables") and because we felt the heart had been torn out of the Vatican II faith by which we were raised. We came to believe that if there really was a Heaven such as described by these religious men with hearts of stone, then they all would be in for a Hell of a surprise.

But we also lost our belief in a Heaven and a Hell in the afterlife, and any sense of a God who granted favors to some and not to others. God became a stranger to us, and an unattractive one at that. We were reintroduced to the divine in Alcoholics Anonymous when we learned to rely on a "higher power" for help in facing our addiction. But with time, the program had very different impacts on Ray's spirituality and on mine. He lost his sense of a "personal"

God, while my experience of a "personal" God increased. If you had shown me a picture in my late thirties and early forties and said, "Find God," I would have known there was something there but I wouldn't have known what to circle.

Not all gay Catholic men have had the same experiences as Ray and me. Many, many years ago, when I wrote and spoke with passion about my beloved Catholicism and my celebrated homosexuality, I was often contacted by other gay men and lesbians who were searching for a way to reconcile their faith with their sexuality. One such visitor was a college student who aspired to be a writer. At the time, he was working on children's literature. I showed him a story I had written about a frog who was ostracized for refusing to make polliwogs, and we reflected on our experiences of the Church.

Thirty years later, he contacted me again to say that we both had been asked to address five hundred nuns, brothers, laypeople, priests, and bishops at the same national conference on "gay people in the Church," and would I like to get together there for a meal. I remembered his name from our first and only meeting but I had never made the connection between him and the celebrated author of *Wicked, Confessions of an Ugly Stepsister,* and *Son of a Witch.* Gregory Maguire told me over Chinese chicken salads in the Minneapolis hotel dining room that he, his partner Andy Newman, and their three adopted children , Luke, Alex, and Helen (a proudly presented wallet photo underscored their beauty) all attended a Catholic Church in Concord, Massachusetts. If it was just Gregory and Andy in the family, their spiritual practice might be different, but Gregory explained that he wanted his children to have the benefit of the religious instruction that had made such a difference in his own development.

Our understanding of God, it would seem, and our ability to see God in the picture of our lives, depends a great deal upon a variety of factors, such as our age, our education, our economic independence, our emotional maturity, our family make-up, our sexual orientation, our gender, our health, our willingness to trust authority, our exposure to other beliefs, and so on.

The exposure to others' beliefs continues to have a profound effect upon Ray's and my spirituality. Being introduced to Buddhism by a Trappist monk friend dramatically altered our experience of life. We began by reading Alan Watts, Thomas Merton, Anthony de Mello, and Jack Kornfield. Our hunger for words that reflected our reality as gay men led us to Thich Nhat Hanh and Pema Chodron. We joined a Sangha and welcomed others to join us in meditation in our home. We learned to bow at the sight of the Buddha and prostrate ourselves before his image in the same way we learned to genuflect in front of the altar and make the sign of the cross with holy water. If you showed us then a picture of our life and asked us to find God, we would have looked to circle the image of the smiling fat man.

Continued practice and daily reading of the 2500-year-old writings of Lao-tzu in the *Tao te Ching* completely changed our focus from the afterlife to this life, from outside us to inside our perceptions of reality. We came to understand that we create our own suffering. That wise lesson has served us well as we work to create a life of love and intimacy together. We also came to understand that the spark of the divine, which our old friend Jesus told us many years ago was within, was available in our encounter with every moment of our day, even in people not waving back, in the dog poop, in the junk mail, in smashed fingers, in the seaweed, in inconsiderate boat operators, in bills, and in barking dogs.

Ray has no investment in an afterlife. He thinks that this life is all there is. His spiritual philosophy can perhaps be summed up in the wise counsel of Meyer Baba who said "Do good and leave the rest to God. Don't worry; be happy." Ray would say though, "Do good and leave the rest to chance," as he doesn't believe in the active hand of a God. Neither do I, but I continue to have the very strong impression of a higher power accompanying me on my walks, as I get a massage, as I have an orgasm, as I make lunch, especially as I swim, as I drive my boat and laugh with delight, as I read and as I pray, and as I watch Ray sleep. It might be an angel. It might be the Holy Spirit. It might be my inner Buddha. I don't know, but I know that it's there.

In the *Tao* it says, "Those who know, don't say. Those who say, don't know."

So, where is God in the picture of my day? I think that I'd really need to circle the whole thing.

147

19

Before departing for what he allegedly hoped would be a lucrative radio talk show career, Ft. Lauderdale, Florida, Mayor Jim Naugle pandered to his Religious Right base with a series of hostile statements about gay people. His words offended me, but not because I believe that everything he said was false. I've made some of the same observations in this book that he did in his press conferences. Rather, I was offended by his motivation, his tone, and his lack of respect for his role as mayor.

I agree that gay people and straight people, as he said, should not use public toilets for sex. There are too few toilets for those of us who have to use them often on the road or in the air. If I see two sets of feet below the stall, I feel as awkward as I do when people engage in loud, personal cell phone conversations nearby. Am I supposed to be quiet? Politely cough to remind them that they have an audience? Hum?

I also agree with him that irresponsible sexual activity leads to increased rates of HIV-infection. That's true for all people, regardless of their orientation, race, or gender.

And when the Mayor explained his practice of using the word "homosexual" because they "aren't gay, they are *unhappy*," I understood why he might feel that many gay men and women are unhappy. Though he and his wife should be so lucky as to be as happy as Ray and me, I also concur that there is a big difference between *gay* people and *homosexuals*.

I don't think the Mayor was saying that people who are unhappy are therefore homosexual, because that would take in most of his socially conservative followers, the grumpy lot with the high incidence of divorce. I think that what he was saying is that unhappy homosexuals aren't *gay*, and I'd amend that by saying if you're *not* happy being gay, then you're a homosexual.

The Republican Senator of Idaho, Larry Craig, who pleaded guilty to disorderly conduct in an airport restroom, repeatedly insisted "I'm *not* gay." No, he's not. He's too unhappy with his sexual orientation to be gay. He's either a *homosexual* or a bisexual, married like millions of others in similar situations around the world, but homosexual or bisexual all the same.

We have lots of specific examples of homosexuals who aren't gay because they're so unhappy with their sexual orientation – Merv Griffin, Ted Haggard, the members of the Vatican Swiss Guard who commit suicide, famous movie stars who become Scientologists, people whose fulltime occupation is to publicly oppose gay civil rights, and those who travel around the country to hold up signs that say "God Hates Fags" – sad, sad, sad homosexuals or bisexuals all.

But Ray and I are not among their number. We are really happy homosexuals, so we're *really, really* gay. It would make us very unhappy to be straight and to have lived a different life than the one we have shared. And what would we call ourselves if we were unhappy straight people? *Heterosexual*? I'll have to call into the Mayor's planned talk show and ask him. Maybe I'll also invite him, if he'd be interested, to look through our photo album and home movies, or sit in on one of our meals with friends. He might get some tips on what happiness really looks like.

We have learned that true, enduring happiness results from a perspective on life, *not* simply from good fortune. Just as we can create our own suffering in life by our desires and our clinging, so too can we create happiness in our lives by letting go of our expectations of perfect and permanent bliss. Ray and I are happy in our lives because we individually have *chosen* to be. That doesn't mean that we don't feel sad, depressed, and angry at times. It means that we try to accept those feelings as important parts of the wonderful experience of life.

That said, there are things which contribute abundantly to our joy. The primary source of Ray's and my happiness is our being together. We hate to be apart. He can't sleep when I'm away. When I'm on a business trip, we talk on the phone daily. And when I'm finished with my presentation, I catch the earliest flight back.

When we're together, we come up with things to do that have the potential to enable us to celebrate life with even more enthusiasm, like galloping on horses through the woods in the beautiful Canadian Rockies or across the golden tundra in Denali National Park in Alaska. We'll white water raft and scream with delight, snorkel for hours and silently point out to each other a beautiful fish that has caught our attention, or jump into the ice cold water at the bottom of the Grand Canyon after riding mules most of the day.

We'll clap with delight like young children when we watch an elephant trumpet a warning when we get too close to her calf on a safari in South Africa, and as our bodies seem to float to the ceiling in San Chapelle as a Parisian choral group sings a cappella. We'll laugh with pure joy when we find ourselves a half an hour ahead of the rest of the group on a three-hour kayaking excursion in the Galapagos, and when we drift in a hot air balloon above the fall foliage around our cabin in New Hampshire.

We'll dance around each other in the kitchen with bliss on Thanksgiving and Christmas as I prepare the turkey, apple-walnut stuffing, mushroom-giblet gravy, rutabaga, garlic mashed potatoes, cranberry sauce, and green beans in rosemary, and while he bakes his two very special pumpkin-pecan pies for the large crowd of friends who join us each holiday. And when they sit down, it will be at a table during Christmas that has been transformed into a magical winter wonderland with slowly moving electric trains, snow-covered trees, elves, colorfully-wrapped chocolates, and candles. What fun we have decorating the house for Christmas, Easter, Halloween, Valentine's Day, and birthdays.

A highlight of our decorating and entertaining joy came over twenty years ago when we filled every inch of our Gloucester, Massachusetts home with greens and poinsettias, hired a caterer and a chamber music quartet, and invited two hundred of our favorite gay, lesbian, and bisexual friends, and straight allies, to an incredible Christmas celebration. Inspired by the old Andre champagne television commercials where the elegant party décor is perfect, we created magic for our community that had been decimated by AIDS and the unresponsive Reagan administration. Our friends,

Congressmen Gerry Studds and Barney Frank, and fundraiser Bob Farmer, mingled gladly with our friends who were hospice workers and antique dealers. Authors Steven McCauley, Neil Miller, Tomie dePaola, and Marcie Hershman exchanged holiday hugs with our friends who sold fireplace equipment and real estate. Highly-acclaimed landscape architect Doug Reed and television newscaster Randy Price shared stories with local political strategists Arlene Isaacson, Richard Burns, and Larry Kessler. Everyone drove over an hour to get there and the laughter, talk, and spontaneously sung Christmas carols lingered with feelings of peace and safety long after the caterers had cleaned up the kitchen and departed.

Ray and I each savor particular memories of delight in our lives, such as walking in St. Mark's Square in Venice slowly eating dark chocolate gelato and listening to the competing orchestras, of finding and filling an extraordinary, homemade dollhouse for a young niece who worried that Santa wouldn't find her if she visited us in Gloucester for the holiday, of packing picnic dinners for our twilight search for deer and moose in the White Mountains of New Hampshire, and of eating fresh blueberry muffins, avocados, hardboiled eggs, and homemade quiche for Easter brunch with my sister and her two grown daughters as we sat on a sweeping hillside in Marin and looked back at our majestic hometown of San Francisco.

Some might argue, "That's easy for you to talk about happiness when you can afford to go on a safari and other exotic vacations, and have a home that would accommodate 200 people." But it's not the setting or the food or the expense of the experience that makes the highlights of our lives memorably happy. Other people could be on the same trips and engage in the same activities and not experience the same happiness. Ray and I *choose* to be in the moment of every experience, even the most ordinary one, to *savor* it, and to let go of our expectations of it. That's what makes us happy. A *grateful* heart wants for nothing. We feel we have *everything* and so we graciously accept whatever else life has to offer.

At every meal we not only give thanks for all that we have that's "good," but also for what's "bad," such as the sore neck or the lingering cold, because they are part of the package, they have lessons to teach us if we are awake, and they remind us of how good it feels to be healthy. We ask that we might be aware of all of the opportunities the day will present us to experience life at its fullest. That can simply be eating Boboli thin crust pizza with homemade toppings at TV tables while watching an episode of *Brothers and Sisters*. Follow that up with a triple chocolate Dove bar and you've got pure heaven.

Ray and I each have sources of happiness that we experience together or separately. For instance, I love to fill the home with interesting art or antiques from every place we visit, to create a garden that blooms throughout the summer, to decorate a room with whimsical objects and old children's toys, to swim in Provincetown Harbor early in the morning before anyone else gets up, or naked at night with only the stars, the moon, and the illuminated Pilgrim Monument to keep me company, to read *Harry Potter* a chapter at a time in bed before falling asleep, to watch in one sitting, with a bowl of popcorn, the three segments of *Lord of the Rings,* to be with our best friends at least every other night to play cards and Mexican Train, to go for leisurely walks after dinner, to look for Christmas presents in July and Christmas wrap in October, to sing songs all day, to make people laugh, to help people make love connections, to act like a six-year-old when I'm with six-year-olds teaching them how to sing "Great Green Gobs of Greasy Grimy Gopher Guts," to stand on the balcony at 5:30 and watch the sun rise over the harbor, to walk the beach in ankle-deep surf, to make pea soup and spaghetti sauce and give it to elderly neighbors, to go to the grocery store and spend time talking with the employees, to think through and prepare a wonderful meal that is shared with friends, to stay on top of the news, to discuss politics, to take the motor boat or my motor bike out on my own, and to make a difference in the world, among other things.

Ray loves to get up by 5 a.m., to have time to himself to drink his coffee and meditate in peace, to read the business section of *The New York Times*, as well as *The Economist* and *Business Week*, to talk at length with our nephew, Jeff, who manages our accounts, to inspect the basements of renovated houses, to putter around the house fixing things that need repair, to wash dishes without interference, to eat dessert, to drink Diet Pepsi, to watch television and go to movies, to enjoy a good mystery, to stay in touch with his nephews, to wash and fold laundry, to spend as much time as he wants at Home Depot and in any hardware store, to do the crossword puzzles in the daily newspapers, to read his book in bed without me talking, to shop on eBay, to manage our finances, to eat leftovers of the food I prepare, to lay in the sun, to laugh at my humor, to play cards if he doesn't lose repeatedly, to save money, to search out wildlife, to walk in the woods, to climb a mountain, and to not be the center of attention, among other things.

We do a lot of compromising to give the other person the optimum opportunity to be happy. For instance, Ray plays cards more than he would probably prefer because he knows that I love to play cards. I sit and work on crossword puzzles with him more than I would prefer because I know he loves to do them together. He goes for walks after dinner with me when he would rather sit and watch television. I try to stay quiet while he's reading in bed even when I have something important to say, which is always. He goes shopping with me even when he has assumed we were done buying things for the house. I watch *South Park* re-runs with him even when I'd rather watch the film *300* again. He lets me buy a fresh Christmas tree every year even though he would rather buy a pre-lit artificial one that would be easier to put up and take down. I let him drive the car even though I get bored riding shotgun. He lets me pick out the restaurant when we travel, even though he'd be happy eating fast food. I let him decide when we're going to stop driving even when I'd like to keep going.

The truth be told, he compromises much more than I do, but that makes us both happy.

This incomplete listing of moments of bliss is not the sole substance of my case, but it is Exhibit A in arguing that the word "gay" can be safely used because some homosexuals are quite happy with their sexual orientation and with the very merry lives we live.

20

Throughout our relationship, which began upon the premise of individual and mutual growth, Ray and I have often asked one another, "If you were to die today, would you have any regrets? Is there anything that you'd like to do that you haven't yet done?"

They are two very different questions. Ray has no regrets today and he feels that there isn't anything he hasn't done that he'd like to do before he dies. His life has been full and rich beyond his wildest expectations. More than his professional success, he has achieved a centeredness and serenity that gives his life great meaning and brings him enormous peace.

He feels he has done right by his family and his friends. He is pleased with the designation of charities to which we have willed our remaining resources upon the occasion of our deaths. He doesn't care about his funeral or about what is done with his remains. He doesn't believe in an afterlife, or in a personal God, and as he doesn't fear death, when his time comes, he will be as ready as is possible to go.

If I precede him in death, he assumes he will stay single, and though he suspects he will eat less well and perhaps laugh less often, he thinks he'll be fine. He knows that he'll immediately sell one of our homes and probably the majority of our possessions. He'll likely travel more, and be content to do that on his own.

Only a handful of, if any, Christmas cards will be sent thereafter. Birthday cards will continue to be mailed only to his brothers and their spouses. He'll rarely answer the phone. He hates to do so now. I imagine him reading lots of books, working lots of crossword puzzles, watching lots of movies (even those that are horrible), continuing with his daily naps, and going to bed and getting up early.

Ray will miss me terribly and it will take him a long time to get over the emptiness and silence in the house. But he will be besieged by friends who will want to take care of him, because he is much loved by everyone who knows him. I imagine he will even hear from friends from the past who pulled away from us because of their disapproving feelings for me, and who now see the opportunity to rebuild their relationships with Ray. He'll be unlikely to respond to their overtures. What they don't realize is that I'm far more forgiving than he is.

I'm different than Ray. I suspect that I will die differently and that I would survive differently, should he precede me in death. Our different "styles," as I like to say, are what, I suspect, helps the relationship work as well as it does and last as long as it has.

Perhaps by age 95, which is how old Ray has anticipated we can live as financially secure as we are now, I will have no regrets and there won't be anything that I feel I haven't done and would like to do.

My regrets today are few. I wish I had been less sassy and smug as a teenager. I was a thoughtful, obedient, and devoted son, but I'm sure that my father might have more enjoyed his dinner after spending a long day at the office and enduring a long commute home had I been more respectful of his and Mom's sacrifices on my behalf. When I witness the way many teenagers today talk to their parents, I cringe with regret that my own rebellion might have come across just as disrespectfully.

I also wish I could have spared my folks, my relatives, my friends, my colleagues at *The Michigan Catholic*, and my partner, Fr. Dan, the turmoil they all felt in their lives with my public coming out in 1974. I don't know how I would have done it differently. I didn't seek the initial publicity, and I feel the ordeal ultimately led us all to a better place, but I wish that the decision of mine to be honest about myself could have been made with less emotional impact on the lives of others.

I also regret, and will even if I live until age 95, the negative impact my careless tongue might have had on the lives of others. Back in grade school, a nun once explained that repeating rumors or saying negative things about others, was like shaking a feather pillow out a window on a windy day. "You'll never be able to find all of the feathers," she cautioned.

In Buddhism, they talk of "right speech." That means that you only speak the truth, and then kindly and only when it will do good. My mother was a wonderful role model for "right speech." I should have learned from her example. But, my fears, doubts, and insecurities have prompted me to "stir the pot," all too frequently, I think. While I have tried hard to manage my tongue, I have often felt the frustration of the saint who cut out his own tongue rather than continue to allow it to possibly cause harm to others.

Have I done everything that I'd like to do? Again, I have now, and will undoubtedly have at the end of my life, some unfinished business. In the often cited example of the mayonnaise jar that has been filled with water and sand, and shaken vigorously, my water is still murky with ego-related busyness. I'm hoping to leave this world more settled and serene than I am now. But other than that, I know that appearing on *Oprah,* or being cited by the *Advocate* as a "hero," won't ultimately make me happy. I feel that I have had a very full and enriched life, spiritually and physically.

Were Ray to die before me, I would grieve terribly but I would probably end up in another relationship eventually. I wouldn't expect the next person to compare with Ray and I would hope not to impose those expectations on him. But I thrive in a relationship. It brings the best out of me. And while I'd like to know that I could find happiness on my own, I think it wouldn't be long before I was again facing the challenges of how to bring two unique personalities together in a new form. It will be a lot harder for me to do so in my later life than it was for me in my late twenties, but I know that nothing good happens without patience, compromise, and hard work, and I'm capable of all three.

Though I'm well aware now of how much I count on Ray, it will shock me how incomplete and useless I will feel if he dies first. I will miss the beautiful smile that greets me each morning in the kitchen, the assortment of vitamins and pills laid out for me on the set table, the open ear I get to the telling of my dreams, my plans for the day, my opinions on all things in the news, and my feelings at the moment.

I will probably start eating my breakfast standing up and won't bother cutting up the fruit for the cereal or smoothie as I now do each morning. I certainly won't fry eggs and bacon on Sunday mornings, nor will I spend time on the crossword puzzle.

I'll do my own dishes, wash my own clothes, vacuum the floors, and scrub the toilet. If the computer doesn't work, I won't know what to do other than to keep hitting keys with the futile hope that I will undo whatever it is that I have mistakenly done. There will be far more repair people at the house than there are today. I'll need someone to attend to electrical and plumbing problems. And if they don't have a television/DVD player/cable box by then that operates by pushing just one button, I'll never watch television again, and not be able to play any of our music.

I'll eat lunch standing up and probably right out of the cottage cheese container. Dinner will be eaten on a TV table – no, wait, if I can't watch TV there's no reason to set up the table. Dinner will be served at the counter too. Beautifully prepared and presented meals will be done for special friends but it will exhaust me. I will have to not only cook, but also to set and clear the table, refill water glasses, wash the dishes, and compliment myself on how good the food was as I reflect alone in bed on the success of the evening.

I'll call people and e-mail them more often. I'll accept more speaking engagements and work assignments. I'll feel less comfortable with gay couples, especially old friends. And I'll probably buy a dog.

I'll cry a lot, especially at night when it's time to see that beautiful smile and kiss those wonderful lips just before I turn off the light. I'll sleep in later because there will be no reason to get up early. I'll go back to AA meetings as a way of being with people who are honest and who understand how I feel. And after a reasonable time, I'll look through our many photo albums, picture by picture, to recall the lifetime of happy memories we shared.

I'll try to learn to sit still with myself. I'll meditate more and take long, long walks. I'll probably find a therapist or a gay men's discussion group, and I'll pour my heart out in a journal.

All of this will happen in the first year. Then I think that I'll be ready to try to love again.

What has just been described as the way each of us would survive the other's death could happen without either of us dying. The relationship could die too and, if it does, we'll reluctantly choose to go in separate directions. If we quit growing individually or as a couple, both of us would feel compelled to initiate a change. We don't see our relationship of love as a marathon. We don't feel that there is a prize for the couple, gay or straight, who stays together the longest. Neither of us imagines or wants to spend eternity with the other, or with anyone else, for that matter. We don't feel we owe it to anyone to stay together unless the relationship continues to work for us. By "work," I mean that it continues to be the vehicle which *enhances* rather than *impedes* our goal of becoming the best Brian McNaught and the best Ray Struble possible.

If we sensed that we were having significant difficulties in the relationship, we would both commit to working hard in couple's counseling, not because it would be so difficult financially to part ways, which is not a good reason to stay together, but because we would feel we owed it to each other and to the life we have built together to try to figure out a way to have the relationship continue to meet both of our needs. That might entail a radical restructuring, and we would each agree to do so if at all possible.

Ray and I live with the possibility of breaking up. We embrace it as an option. Doing so gives our relationship a vitality it would otherwise lack. Just as embracing death makes one's life more meaningful, so too does the option of separating make us better appreciate the unique love life we have created together.

I suspect, and hope, that we will grow old(er) together. That would suit me just fine. Ideally, we will die at the same moment, so that neither of us has to bear the loss of the other. But that doesn't often happen with couples. One of us will have to endure the terrible pain.

Neither Ray nor I, as I have said before, are perfect people, nor is our relationship perfect. But we work for each other and the relationship works for us. I bless the day that he crossed the street and climbed into my car in 1976, ready to guide me to our new home and ultimately to our new life together. I bless the choices we have made to stay together throughout these many years despite the obstacles we have faced, created by others and by ourselves.

We have tried very hard to build worlds for each other where we both feel very safe and very valued. Our homes have been decorated with rich reminders of our mutual journey and with whimsical touchstones of our youth. We have shielded ourselves to the best of our ability from the cynicism of others, both gay and straight, and from the conscious and deliberate efforts of the Vatican and of socially conservative politicians and ministers to undermine our relationship.

We two formerly middle-class, Midwestern, Irish Catholic gay men from families of seven, have endured a great deal in order to love one another as intimate spouses. It has often been a lonely, frightening path as we were buffeted by hostility in our families, our neighborhoods, our Church, our places of employment, and in our country. We have wounds from the hurtful things that have been said and done to us by people who were horrified by, or jealous of, our same-sex intimacy.

But we have also been helped along the way by family members, neighbors, and people of faith, by colleagues, and by friends. Many people who are gay, lesbian, bisexual, and heterosexual worldwide have encouraged us with their kindness and their generosity. In a thousand surprising moments, individuals known and unknown to us have nurtured us physically and spiritually in hospital emergency rooms, AA meetings, airport customs lines, at nudist camps and at Mass, in gay pride parades and in corporate board rooms, with what they wrote in cards, e-mails, books, on top of chocolate cakes, in editorials and letters to the editor, in donations and phone calls made and in votes cast, in speeches given and in marriage certificates signed, in apologies offered and in congratulations sent. The good has *far* outweighed the bad, the positive has far outweighed the negative, and the support has far outweighed the opposition.

Our relationship did not happen all at once. It *became*. Just like the Skin Horse explained to the Velveteen Rabbit, it takes a long time to make something *real*. That's why it doesn't often happen to people who "break easily," or who have "sharp edges," or who have to be "carefully kept." Generally, by the time a relationship is real, most of your hair has been loved off, and your eyes drop out, and you get loose in the joints, and very shabby. But those things don't matter at all, because once your relationship is *real*, you can't be ugly, except to people who don't understand.

If you look closely today, really closely, at the photos of Ray and me as youngsters and at the one of us in an intimate embrace after many years of loving one another, you'll see the same beautiful smiles (and chubby cheeks) of innocence. Our hair is now grayer and there are wrinkles on our faces, but we once again feel cherished. We still don't look alike, but people continue to sense a relationship that they want to figure out. We're not biological brothers with grins of delight, but we're *logical* brothers who have helped each other regain a sense of being adored. We see it in our faces, young and old. We also feel it in our hearts. If you don't see it or feel it, take another look. It's there. I promise.

ABOUT THE AUTHOR

Brian McNaught is a sexuality trainer and author whose primary focus are the issues facing gay, lesbian, bisexual, and transgender people, and those who live and work with them. Named "the godfather of gay diversity training," by *The New York Times*, he has worked primarily with heterosexual audiences in major corporations and university settings throughout the world since 1974. His six books and six DVDs are used extensively in classrooms and board rooms internationally. He served as the Mayor of Boston's Liaison to the Gay Community, and currently serves as an advisor to former Surgeon General David Satcher on matters of national sexual health. He and his spouse Ray Struble divide their year between Provincetown, MA and Ft. Lauderdale, FL. To contact Brian or to learn more about his work, please go to www.brian-mcnaught.com.

LaVergne, TN USA
13 June 2010
185872LV00002BA/36/P